Pergolas

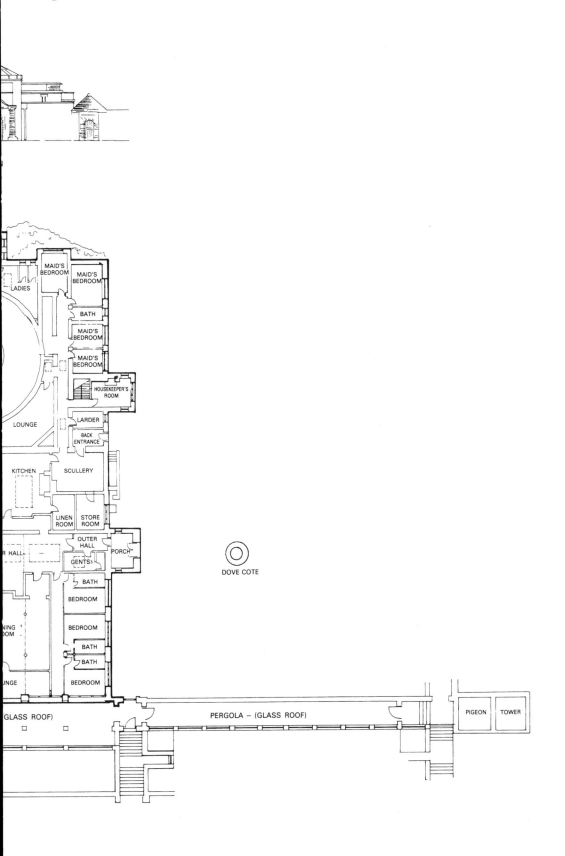

MAID'S BEDROOM

MAID'S BEDROOM

LADIES

BATH

MAID'S BEDROOM

MAID'S BEDROOM

HOUSEKEEPER'S ROOM

LARDER

LOUNGE

BACK ENTRANCE

KITCHEN

SCULLERY

LINEN ROOM

STORE ROOM

OUTER HALL

PORCH

R HALL

GENTS

BATH

BEDROOM

NING OM

BEDROOM

BATH

BATH

UNGE

BEDROOM

DOVE COTE

GLASS ROOF)

PERGOLA – (GLASS ROOF)

PIGEON

TOWER

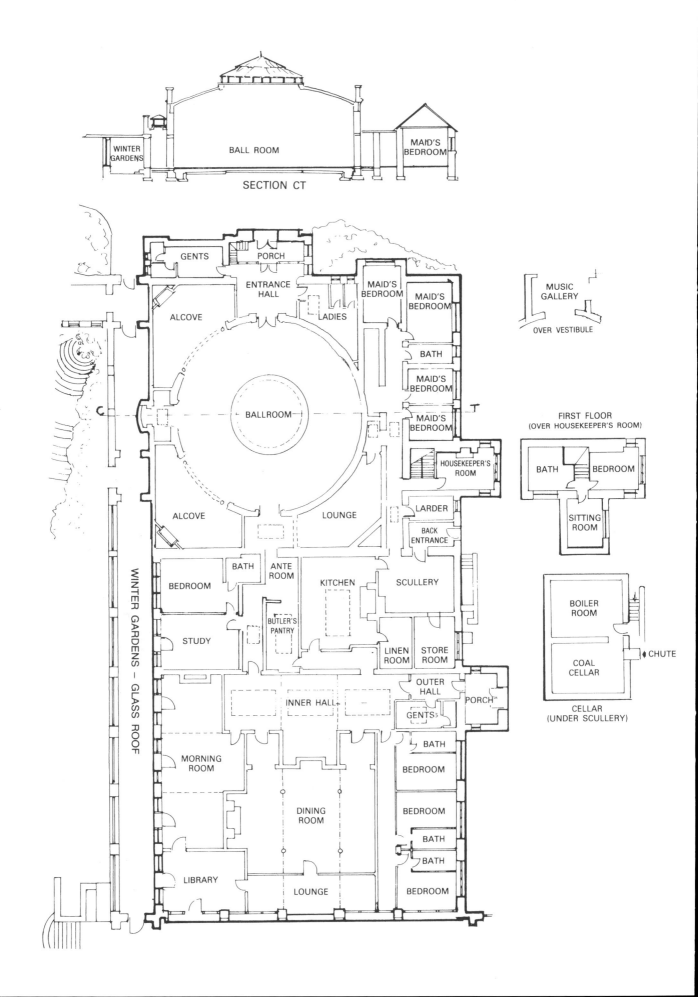

SECTION CT

WINTER GARDENS

BALL ROOM

MAID'S BEDROOM

GENTS

PORCH

ENTRANCE HALL

MAID'S BEDROOM

MAID'S BEDROOM

MUSIC GALLERY

OVER VESTIBULE

ALCOVE

LADIES

BATH

MAID'S BEDROOM

FIRST FLOOR
(OVER HOUSEKEEPER'S ROOM)

BALLROOM

MAID'S BEDROOM

BATH

BEDROOM

ALCOVE

LOUNGE

HOUSEKEEPER'S ROOM

SITTING ROOM

LARDER

BACK ENTRANCE

BATH

ANTE ROOM

KITCHEN

SCULLERY

BOILER ROOM

BEDROOM

BUTLER'S PANTRY

CHUTE

STUDY

LINEN ROOM

STORE ROOM

COAL CELLAR

WINTER GARDENS – GLASS ROOF

OUTER HALL

CELLAR
(UNDER SCULLERY)

INNER HALL

GENTS

PORCH

BATH

MORNING ROOM

BEDROOM

BEDROOM

DINING ROOM

BATH

BATH

LIBRARY

LOUNGE

BEDROOM

LEVERHULME'S RIVINGTON

(The story of the Rivington 'Bungalow')

M.D.Smith

Front Cover   *Water colour painting of the second Bungalow by Jill M. Aldersley of Ambleside, Cumbria; surmounted by photographs of Lord Leverhulme and his armorial bearings.*

Inside Front Cover   *Plan of the lay-out of the second Bungalow.*

Author's Note

Leverhulme's Rivington was first published in March 1984 and subsequently reprinted in 1992. The present work contains many additional illustrations and copy documents some of which have only come to light since the original publication. A section containing coloured photographs is also included to facilitate comparisons, together with information which updates the story.

The Author

The author, Malcolm David Smith, was born at Coppull, Near Chorley, on 4th January 1943. He lives in Adlington with his wife, Andrea, and two sons, Ian and Paul. Following primary and secondary education at Coppull Moor C of E School and Chorley Grammar School, respectively; David (which is the name he prefers) joined the Lancashire Constabulary as a police cadet being stationed at Chorley. He was appointed a constable in January 1962 and remained in the Police Service all his working life. Following various postings to places as diverse as Lytham-St.Annes, Wigan and Manchester City Centre, he retired on the 31st December 1993 while serving as the prosecutions/licensing inspector at Bolton Central. A long interest in local history occupies much of his time. Other books include the histories of Horwich, Blackrod, Rivington, Adlington and the Locomotive Works at Horwich.

Typesetting by Highlight Type Bureau Ltd, Bradford
Printed by The Amadeus Press Ltd, Huddersfield

Wyre Publishing
North Villas, St. Michael's on Wyre, Lancashire, PR3 OTE0

ISBN number 0-9526187-3-7

Copyright © 1998.

"Ruins Yet Beauteous in Decay"
(Robert Burns 1759 - 1796)

Dedicated to the memory of

William Mason (14.9.1906 - 9.3.1983)

and his wife Ida Mason (nee Fairclough)

William and Ida Mason, 1940.

View of the front of 'The Bungalow' from the main driveway. Note the dovecote and second storey which date it after the ballroom was built. Stones on the left were for the construction of a rockery about 1930.

ACKNOWLEDGEMENTS

I wish to thank all those who have assisted me in any way whatsoever in the compilation of this work and without wishing to detract from the efforts of those not specifically mentioned I owe especial thanks to the following:-

My wife Andrea and her brother Paul Barry Mason without whose help, and encouragement I doubt the work would ever have been completed.

MISS JILL M. ALDERSLEY . . . . .North Road, Ambleside, Cumbria (Cover)

* FRED ASHWORTH . . . . .Pall Mall Cottages, Rivington.

AILSA BOWERS . . . . .Port Sunlight Information Centre.

MARTIN BROWNLOW . . . . .Twig End, Rivington..

KEVIN CAMPBELL . . . . .Bolton Library Archivist.

MRS. CORNTHWAITE . . . . .Higher Kit Brow, Ellel, Galgate.

ANTHONY CUBBERLEY . . . . .Oak Lane, Sevenoaks, Kent.

MRS. DOROTHY DARBYSHIRE. . . . . .Babylon Lane, Heath Charnock.

* HAROLD DICKINSON . . . . .Lever Park Avenue, Horwich.

GEOFFREY FAIRBROTHER . . . . .Crown Lane, Horwich.

* MRS. PHYLLIS HAWORTH . . . . .Woodland Drive, Warton, Nr. Preston.

MR. & * MRS. G. KAY . . . . .Victoria Road, Horwich.

MISS DOROTHY KERSHAW . . . . .Major Bottoms, Anderton.

MR. JACK KINGS . . . . .Ainslie Road, Bolton.

* MRS. IDA MASON . . . . .Babylon Lane, Anderton.

MRS. VIOLET PENDLEBURY . . . . .Ladycrosse Drive, Whittle-le-Woods.

MRS. G. M. SARGENT . . . . .Fifth Avenue, Bolton.

BRIAN SMITH . . . . .Ardley Road, Horwich.

JOHN SMITH . . . . .Harts House, Horwich.

* KEITH SHONE . . . . .Westgate Avenue, Bolton.

(* deceased)

ADDITIONAL ACKNOWLEDGEMENTS

The undermentioned have been of assistance with the compilation of the present re-issue of the book:-

KENNETH DICKINSON . . . . .Chorley Old Road, Horwich.

MILDRED GILHOOLY . . . . .Sutton Lane, Adlington.

PATRICIA HEYES . . . . .Bolton Road, Anderton.

KEVIN SALMON . . . . .Rivington Hall, Rivington.

MARY SHONE . . . . .Pocket Nook Road, Lostock.

TOM LORD . . . . .Lytham Road, Fulwood.

BOLTON EVENING NEWS . . . .

CONTENTS

Rivington Village Green and Post Office from Sheep House Lane. (Circa 1905).

Rivington Village and Green, circa 1950.

FOREWORD

The picturesque village of Rivington remains virtually unspoiled despite being situated in Lancashire's industrial heartland. The expansion of trade in the mid nineteenth century, particularly from the Port of Liverpool, seems to have contributed, indirectly, to this circumstance. Increase in the population of the city, plus a new awakening in awareness of sanitation and cleanliness, resulted in the Corporation of Liverpool looking for a source of pure, clean water for its residents. The wells used in the city were less than hygienic and there was a high incidence of cholera and typhoid.

The water catchment area on the moors above Rivington was harnessed to feed a series of reservoirs which were constructed in the valley below. The original supply of water was coloured brown and tainted but these initial shortcomings soon disappeared and the supply became reputed for its clarity and purity. Thenceforth Liverpool Corporation have carefully monitored the number and type of buildings which were constructed on its holdings, with the specific purpose of preventing pollution of the water supply, and have thus preserved the area from the attention of the industrialist and property developer.

Over the years, since the construction of the reservoirs, nature has mellowed and camouflaged the effect of man's hand and the 'Rivington Lakes' form part of the enchanting beauty of this place. On the barren slopes of the moorland, rising above the reservoirs, there once existed a palatial residence surrounded by landscaped garden areas of breathtaking beauty.

Traces of the once magnificent 'Bungalow' can still be seen and there is ample evidence of the scale of the grounds in the tumble-down remains of summer houses and stone pathways. There is a sadness about the place for me, as when something beautiful is lost for ever, and my purpose in writing this book is an attempt to recreate a realistic impression of how the 'Bungalow' looked in its hey-day.

The Bungalow, Rivington, Lancashire, was the mountain home of William Hesketh Lever, the first Viscount Leverhulme, a native of Bolton, who founded the still successful firm of Lever Brothers Limited. It is indicative of the popularity of this residence that many post card views still exist and a selection of these, plus photographs and information from various other sources have provided the foundation for this work.

The research and collection of pertinent information has provided a worthwhile, interesting and stimulating exercise. If the reader derives a like amount of pleasure from the following pages I shall be more than rewarded for my efforts.

Malcolm David Smith
27 Sutton Lane, Adlington
Lancashire PR6 9PA
1983

Rivington Lakes

INTRODUCTION

My intention is not to produce an exhaustive, detailed study of 'The Bungalow', because there is a natural loathing of technical books but more a chronological story, illustrated by a collection of photographs, which I am sure will achieve more than the text. There are certain inherent difficulties in separating events into 'time bands' as, for instance, 'Roynton Cottage' and 'The Bungalow' existed between specific dates whilst Lever Park and the Bungalow Grounds were constructed over a long period of time, as will become clear.

I have experienced some difficulty in collecting information because whilst people are generally quite prepared to recount experiences or reminisce, there has been a marked reluctance to part with possession of material even for copying purposes. I met this type of obstruction on several occasions and the underlying reason was that those persons were afraid that the articles loaned would be lost or not returned to them which has apparently happened previously. Whilst mishaps do occur it is obvious that all the occasions were not accidental and whoever was responsible has rendered an extreme disservice. One can appreciate that a photograph for instance which has been in a family for a number of generations has a great sentimental value and can be irreplaceable.

I have been fortunate enough to enjoy excellent co-operation from a number of people whose names I have included in the acknowledgement list. Without assistance an undertaking of this nature is impossible and it would be naive to think otherwise. The list does not include all those persons to whom I am indebted for help because it is not practicable to obtain details of Library and Museum staff who are generally helpful in the course of their work.

Working on the adage, 'procrastination is the thief of time' I decided at the outset that on reaching a situation where the intelligence I was receiving was becoming repetitive, it could well be because the information which was readily available had become exhausted. If there was then sufficient material to produce a cogent, chronological narrative this must be the optimum time to complete it. There is no doubt that there is much more known about the place and a lot of photographic illustrations exist which will remain hidden, having been forgotten, or their significance has just not been realised, nevertheless I feel that there is sufficient included to afford the reader a reasonable impression and understanding of this interesting part of our local history.

The Friday preceding Easter Day is 'Good Friday' which is held as the anniversary of the Crucifixion of Our Lord on the cross at Calvary. It is an established custom among Christians to visit a high area of land on the anniversary of this date in token remembrance of Christ's suffering for us. The local venue for this annual pilgrimage is Rivington Pike.

Thousands of visitors roam the moors on Good Friday and many of them climb to the Pike Tower, an achievement in itself because, standing over one thousand feet above sea level, the Pike is officially classed as a mountain. I often went there as a boy, usually in a group, from the village of Coppull where I lived. We invariably got lost on the way but we always managed to arrive, not too difficult considering that you can see the 'Pike' for miles around. I used to enjoy playing in 'The Bungalow' grounds which we knew as the 'Chinese Gardens'. Stories existed that there used to be a man who lived in a bungalow there but it was of very little interest to me either at that time or for some considerable period thereafter.

Living in close proximity to Rivington and seeing the bleak hills with their prominent landmarks in all seasons the familiarity does not breed contempt but inspires an affection which is difficult to describe. My interest in the moorland's secret was kindled by this affection and who could resist a 'mystery on the doorstep' so to speak.

Arthur Ollerton of Blackrod with his daughter, Vivienne, at Rivington Pike on a Good Friday during the 1950's.

View of Rivington Pike across the Upper Rivington Reservoir. Crica 1905. Rivington Church is in the centre of the picture with the vicarage far left. Roynton Cottage is on the skyline, top left.

Landmarks on the Moors above Rivington Village, left to right:
1. *Independent Broadcasting Transmitter Mast - Winter Hill.*
2. *Pigeon Tower and Bungalow Grounds.*
3. *Pike Tower.*

Chapter 1 - Landmarks

On a clear day, when mist or low cloud does not hide them from view, there are three distinct landmarks visible on the moors above Rivington Village.

The tallest and most striking is the Winter Hill Transmitter Station Mast towering above the Independent Broadcasting Authority Station on Winter Hill. The main mast has a number of sister masts adjacent to it but these are not always evident when viewed from the lowlands. At night time a series of red marker lamps arranged at intervals along its height are illuminated as a warning to aircraft.

Winter Hill is the highest point of the moors rising to almost 1,500 feet. In ancient times it was used as a site for certain religious ceremonies as Baines 'History of Lancashire' records:-

"The people assembled in Rivington to celebrate public worship in the open air at a place called Winter Hill, which, from its amphitheatrical form, exalted the congregation to hear the solemn truths thundered from the stone pulpit, which stood in its centre".

In more recent times a tragic aircrash occurred there on Thursday 27th February 1958, when a passenger plane flying from the Isle of Man to Manchester crashed into the hillside, in appalling weather conditions, killing all but seven of the forty two passengers and crew aboard.

The second landmark and by far the oldest is the watchtower on Rivington Pike. During the reign of Henry VIII (1509 - 1547) Rivington Pike was described by Leland as follows:-

"one part of this Hille when I saw it first is called Faierlokke, but communely the people thereabout caulleth it Riven pike";

and he adds,

"There was a Coppe in the Hille, as a backe standing up above the residue of the Hille".

The 'coppe' was the site of an ancient beacon, one in a chain extending the length and breadth of England, maintained for the purpose of sending messages of alarm in times of danger. (The building of the Beacon Tower on Rivington Pike - G. N. Shawcross).

The earliest mention of the beacon on Rivington Pike dates back to 1588 when during the reign of Elizabeth I, whilst England was threatened by invasion from the Spanish Armada; the fleet assembled by Phillip II of Spain for the conquest of this country, the beacon site was continually manned for several months - "to appraise the inhabitants of the approach of the invaders and to rouse into action their most vigorous efforts". The cost of manning the site was shared between the divisions of Manchester, Bolton and Middleton. (Baines History of Lancashire).

Rivington Pike Tower circa 1880 from a photograph by Luke Berry of Chorley. (Note Chimney). Seated in front are Mrs. Margaret Evelyn Crompton with her two sons Andrews and Theodore. John William Crompton is standing in the centre of the group to the left. This family occupied Rivington Hall until 1910.

Left: Rivington Pike Watch Tower, Circa 1900.

Below: Rivington Pike Fell Race, 1959.

The Pigeon Tower showing the screening wall, 1998.

Rivington Lakes provide the background for this photograph of the Pigeon Tower taken from the east, 1998.

There is a fireplace in the top room of the Pigeon Tower which is shown above. The significance of the circular design is that the initials W.H.E.E.L. refer to William Hesketh and Elizabeth Ellen Lever. Lord Leverhulme's motto contained in his armorial bearings is MUTARE VEL TIMERE SPERNO (To change or to fear I spurn).

Winter Hill Transmitter Station, 1985. On the left of the photograph can be seen the Scotsman's Post, a pillar erected to commemorate the murder of George Henderson near the spot on the 9th November 1838.

*Close-up views of the
Scotsman's Post, c.1910 and 1990.*

*Below: Winter Hill television mast reaches
high above the moorland.*

A number of communications masts are situated close to the main Winter Hill mast.

Cattle herded together for warmth below Winter Hill.

The present watchtower was built in 1733 and stones from the ancient beacon were incorporated at the base of the construction. A story is attached to the building of the present tower which is briefly as follows:-

In 1729 John Andrews of Little Lever, Bolton, who owned one half of the Manor of Rivington, by descent, purchased the other half from one John Breres for the sum of £1,747.

The landlord of adjoining property, Christopher Horrocks, had proceedings brought against two of Andrews's employees for allegedly taking and detaining a cow at a place called Wildersmoor on the 17th March 1733.

The dispute centred on where the moor boundary lay between the respective properties of Andrews and Horrocks. The two accused Andrew's employees were strenuously defended by Andrews's legal representatives. Litigation became both protracted and costly and in the event the action was dismissed in 1737 after three hearings at the Assizes. The outcome however resulted in the moor boundary between the parishes of Rivington and Horwich being properly defined.

John Andrews commenced negotiations with local stonemasons to build the present watchtower on 17th June 1732. The accounts for the building work published by Shawcross make interesting reading. For example:-

May 1733 - paid James Gill for making cellar - 17 daies and ¹/₂ and he is to doe one day more at covering the Sough for that wage - £1-0s-5d.

The Beacon Tower is 20 ft. high and 17 ft. square externally. The interior is a single chamber 13 ft. square and a fireplace was included in one corner. Entrance was on the east side and there were wall windows. Cellar accommodation was 5 ft. deep by 3 ft. square under the 3" thick flag floor which was supported by stone buttresses. It may be said that John Andrews erected the tower as evidence of legal ownership of the moor.

The structure was intended as a hunting lodge and the protective warmth it afforded against the bitter winds will no doubt have been most welcome to the hunters. During 1933 when Shawcross wrote his article on the tower he recorded that the exterior of the building had been recently pointed and was in good condition although the roof had decayed and over half the covering had fallen into the main chamber. A few years ago the dangerous state of the watchtower prompted discussion on the advisability of having it demolished but following a public outcry, Chorley Rural District Council took over the responsibility to renovate and preserve it for posterity.

Looking at the western slopes of Rivington Moor there is a roughly square shaped area of dense vegetation covering a section of the hillside laterally and extending almost to the summit of the moor. This concentration of trees and shrubs stands out as dark green against the paler hues of the coarse shrubs and grasses which cover the remainder of these uplands and appears incongruous to the observer. The explanation is that within the perimeter of this area stood 'The Bungalow' set in 45 acres of beautifully landscaped gardens, which dwelling has been described as "one of the most attractive small residential properties in the North of England".

In the top left hand corner of this square of vegetation standing like a lonely sentinel silhouetted against the skyline, is the third of these landmarks, the 'Pigeon Tower'.

The barren and inhospitable spot chosen by Lord Leverhulme as the site for his residence identified the need for animation to dispel the feeling of loneliness. This was introduced by building bird houses throughout the grounds, whose feathered inhabitants cheered up the place with their constant comings and goings amidst a cacophony of sound.

The 'Pigeon Tower' was built as a 'look out' and loggia were constructed below it with observation plateaux to take advantage of the panoramic views afforded from this altitude. Adjoining the tower was an arched opening with a screen 250 ft. long containing pigeon holes which relieve the otherwise unbroken face from monotony.

Of Italian design this 'Rapunzel' tower has rooms at three levels, access being gained by a winding stone staircase which runs up the semi-circular spine of the building. The two lower rooms were bird houses but the top floor was decked out as a small sitting room with a fireplace. Lady Leverhulme is supposed to have spent many hours in the 'pigeon tower' sewing and playing musical instruments, not very well though I am told.

That anyone should contemplate living in these wild and rugged surroundings, let alone conceive the idea of constructing garden areas, where even the hardy moorland shrubs and grasses barely managed to exist, seems totally incomprehensible; but all of this and even more was eventually achieved, principally due to the vision and courage of a singularly brilliant individual. William Hesketh Lever; a native of Bolton to whom I shall refer more fully in subsequent chapters.

The Pigeon Tower stands above the loggia and the boating lake. Lord Leverhulme sometimes went for a swim in this small lake.

Chapter 2 - Rivington Hall Estate

Although Rivington is not specifically mentioned in the 'Domesday Book' there is little doubt that it existed as a manor before the Norman Conquest in 1066. In the Great Inquest of 1212 reference is made to 'RUHWINTON' in the Salford Hundred which was held in 'thanage' by Alexander Pilkington. The title 'Ruhwinton' is an early name from which 'Rivington' was derived. A 'thane' incidentally, in the Anglo-Saxon community was a member of the class intermediate between tenant farmers and the nobility. His property was held on condition of military service and required the payment of a nominal annual rent of a few shillings to the Crown.

The illustrious Pilkington family fought at the Battle of Bosworth Field during the Wars of the Roses, and were almost wiped out, have contributed much to the history of Rivington. Their family crest includes a man with a scythe and the motto "NOW THUS - NOW THUS" which is an allusion to one of the family who, in order to escape his enemies, disguised himself as a mower. Richard Pilkington was responsible for building the first Rivington Church and his son James, who was born in 1518, became Bishop of Durham, the first Protestant prelate of this see.

The Non Conformists of Rivington built a Chapel for themselves in 1703 where they could be a united congregation, free to manage their own affairs, and, above all, free to worship God according to the dictates of conscience.

Robert Pilkington was the last Lord of the Manor of Rivington from that family. He is reported to have borrowed considerable sums of money on the security of his lands and by his will, dated 16th November 1605, he left the estate in trust to three executors who transferred it to the mortgagees in settlement of the debts. Robert Lever of D'arcy Lever and Thomas Breres of Preston, bought out the various claimants and between them acquired the Rivington Estate. The two property holders passed their lands to surviving issue until; as previously mentioned, John Andrews bought out the other remaining tenant in 1729.

In 1834 Lucy Fletcher, a descendant of John Andrews, married Woodhouse Crompton of Bolton and thus the name of Crompton enters the lineage. Their son John William Crompton married and the couple had two sons, Andrews and Theodore. During the 1890's this family decided to sell Rivington Estate and R. Cecil Winders, Solicitors of Bolton were engaged to act in the negotiations.

Coincidentally Lord Leverhulme was on the 'look out' for a suitable property in the area and on hearing that Rivington Hall Estate was on the market he was immediately interested in purchasing the lands. He had loved the moors since his childhood days and had enjoyed many happy hours there during his courtship with Lady Leverhulme.

In January 1900, Lord Leverhulme instructed a local firm of solicitors, F. W. Thompson Esq., of Wood Street, Bolton to negotiate the purchase of Rivington Manor. An opening offer of £40,000 was made but this was rejected as being nothing approaching the sum that was acceptable to the vendor. As the initial offer was rejected Winders were asked to provide a valuation figure for the estate which was eventually put at £70,000 and the sale included an agreement that John Crompton could occupy Rivington Hall, at an agreed annual rental, and his wife, and eldest son Andrews after him, if they so desired.

Objections were made to Andrews continuing in residence, for obvious reasons, and following the withdrawal of this condition Lord Leverhulme's solicitors made a firm bid of £60,000 which was accepted on the 23rd March 1900.

Photograph taken outside Rivington Hall circa 1908 showing Andrews Crompton with Mrs. Crompton (on right) and a maid servant holding the Crompton children.

Rivington Hall. Circa 1910.

Rear portion of Rivington Hall.
Circa 1910.

OLD PORTION, RIVINGTON HALL.

Rivington Hall. Circa 1920.

A photograph of Rivington Hall dated 1928.

This view of the hall is dated 26th August 1935.

Substantial re-furbishment work took place to the hall and barns over recent years and this shows some of the extent of those alterations.

Rivington Hall circa 1910. The Mulligan family pictured outside the Hall.

The formalities were concluded and Lord Leverhulme became Baron of Rivington Manor whilst the Crompton family retained occupation of Rivington Hall, including the stable and coach-house; Sweetloves Cottage, Sheephouse Cottage and a vegetable garden near Fisher House, for a yearly rental of £100.

In studying the correspondence concerning this transaction, which is held in Bolton Library Archives, one sentence suggests that John Crompton was unaware of the prospective purchaser and this seems to have been done in an effort to obtain the estate at the most reasonable price. Had Crompton known that Lord Leverhulme was the prospective buyer he may well have insisted on the full asking price of £70,000, knowing that the latter could well afford it. The sentence which I am referring to appears in the letter of acceptance and reads:-

"Is there any reason now why your client's name should not be disclosed to Mr. Crompton. We should like to do so".

The Rivington Hall Estate extended over 2,100 acres and included the manorial seat (Rivington Hall), a number of farmstead holdings, two Anglo Saxon tithe barns and, of course, the watchtower.

Successive tenants had rebuilt the hall on two occasions. Firstly in 1480 when Robert Pilkington built himself a more spacious abode, quadrangular in shape and constructed of timber and plasterwork; and secondly in 1780 when this building had decayed to such an extent that it was demolished and replaced by the existing Manor House.

Lord Leverhulme's agreement to rent the Hall means that he must have intended to build an alternative residence and the site chosen for it, at 1,000 feet above sea level, on the western slopes of the moorland, is reputed to be a favourite picnic spot which he regularly visited with his wife-to-be during their courtship days. No account seems to have been taken of the vicious winds which can assail this elevated spot. It was an aspect probably viewed as unimportantly as it was during those halcyon days of early romance.

A better understanding of Lord Leverhulme's motivation to build a home on that lonely fell side is achieved by a study of the antecedents and character of this remarkable man.

"It is my hope, and my brother's hope, some day to build houses in which our workpeople will be able to live and be comfortable – semi-detached houses, with gardens back and front, in which they will be able to know more about the science of life than they can in a back slum, and in which they will learn there is more in life than the mere going to and returning from work and looking forward to Saturday night to draw their wages." – Viscount Leverhulme (then Mr. W. H. Lever), at the cutting of the first sod of Port Sunlight, 3rd March, 1888.

Photograph of Lord Leverhulme , 1921.

Chapter 3 - William Hesketh Lever

William Hesketh Lever was born in Bolton on the 19th September 1851, the eldest of two sons in a family of ten children.

His mother and father were hard working people who ran a thriving wholesale grocery business in Bank Street, Bolton. They were strict Non-Conformists, totally opposed to drink or gambling but nevertheless the family enjoyed a happy childhood and were devoted to their parents.

William received his primary education at a small private school in Wood Street, Bolton, a pleasant Georgian cul-de-sac where the family home was also situated. The school took boys until they were turned nine and girls up to sixteen years of age. The friendships which William formed at this establishment were to remain throughout his life, he had the good fortune to enjoy the companionship of his school friends in old age.

Educationally speaking William was not the most gifted pupil but he proved to be quick witted, resourceful, orderly minded and diligent, with a keen interest in sport, particularly swimming. He left school when he was sixteen years old, his last school attended being a Church of England concern; which was a little unusual considering the religious persuasion of his parents. On leaving school he was taken into the family business being treated without preference and paid the 'going rate' of one shilling per week for cutting up the long bars of soap into manageable sized pieces and wrapping them in waxed paper.

Involvement in the day to day workings of the family enterprise caused William to react against his father's business conservatism. He suggested a number of administrative and procedural changes to improve efficiency which were initially viewed with some misgivings but on their being implemented they proved to be of great benefit.

A single and relatively insignificant sixteenth birthday gift had a deep and lasting effect on William. He was given a copy of the book 'Self Help' by Samuel Smiles which had been first published in November 1859. The book contains a series of anecdotes concerning the lives of such people as Richard Cobden, Robert Peel, Isambard Kingdom Brunel and Lord Nelson.

The message which this work conveys is that all things can be achieved by purposeful application and economical usage of 'time'. The point is emphasised in that the famous personages mentioned have made their mark in history despite their upbringings, which were often in poor and deprived circumstances, and the constant trials and tribulations encountered in the quest for success. I have read a copy of the book which a little 'dry' but the quotations, two of which are reproduced below, when read in conjunction with the biographies, are very valid:-

Portrait of Sir William Hesketh Lever Bt. by George Hall Neale.

"An economical use of time is the best method of securing leisure: it enables us to get through business and carry it forward, instead of being driven by it. On the other hand, the miscalculation of time involves us in perpetual hurry, confusion and difficulties; and life becomes a mere shuffle of expedients, usually followed by disaster". Nelson once said, "I owe all my success in life to having been always a quarter of an hour before my time".

"Useful and instructive though good reading may be, it is only one mode of cultivating the mind and is much less influential than practical experience and good example in the formation of character".

Lord and Lady Leverhulme

Lever Brothers original soap works at Warrington.

Wharf and Docks at Port Sunlight.

Barges laden with soap at Port Sunlight Docks.

Bars of soap drying at Port Sunlight.

Cutting up bars of soap at Port Sunlight.

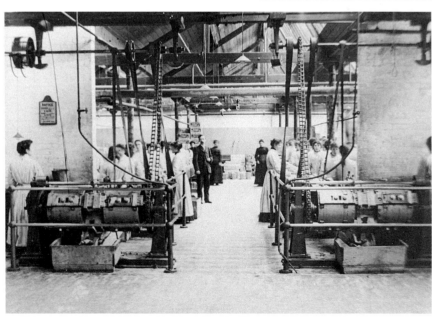

Stamping bars of soap at Port Sunlight.

*First Cottages built in Port Sunlight.
A Reproduction awarded Grand Prix
at the Brussels Exhibition. 1910.*

Nailing soap boxes at Port Sunlight.

Port Sunlight Fire Brigade.

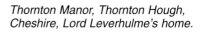
Thornton Manor, Thornton Hough, Cheshire, Lord Leverhulme's home.

THE MANOR. THORNTON HOUGH

Music Room at Thornton Manor.

LEWIS CASTLE, STORNOWAY.

Lewis (or Lews) Castle, Stornoway, which was once owned by Lord Leverhulme.

Ball Room at Lewis Castle.

Whaling Station, Harris. 1923. Lord Leverhulme promoted many successful enterprises in Harris.

753/84

Hall i'th Wood, Bolton, the home of Samuel Crompton – inventor of the 'spinning mule' – which was re-furbished as a museum by Lord Leverhulme.

The meteoric rise from the situation of grocer's assistant, cutting up the long bars of soap into saleable size pieces and wrapping them, to being the owner of an internationally successful business concern with a multi million pound annual turnover is too well chronicled to dwell on the mechanics of how the success was achieved.

William Hesketh Lever seized upon the idea of producing soap of the highest quality with the brand name 'Sunlight' and pursued this idea with unremitting assiduity, surmounting all obstacles along the way. The branches of his soap combine eventually extended to all parts of the world and he was personally and directly involved in their being set up, financed and successfully administered.

Everyone has heard of Port Sunlight the industrial village set up be Lord Leverhulme during 1888. The first sod for the village was cut by Lady Leverhulme with a silver spade, in March of that year, and this ceremony was followed by a celebration banquet at the Bear's Paw Restaurant in Liverpool. By January 1889 soap production had commenced at the new factory.

Although the roadways in the village were constructed long before the days of motoring the principal ones were 36 ft. wide with 12 ft. pavements on each side. A variety of architects were commissioned to design the houses in 'Old English' style. Residences were widely spaced and well appointed with all modern conveniences. It was a condition of tenancy that the person either worked for Lever Brothers or was entitled to a house for some special reason arising out of the business. The village is as interesting today as it ever was and I must say that I enjoyed my visit there whilst researching this undertaking.

The fruits of his labour were vast but he was a generous man evinced by the numerous benefactions he made of which it would be impossible to give an exhaustive list. His intimate association with Bolton meant that the township benefited in several ways. Bolton School was the outcome of a £100,000 gift from Lord Leverhulme in 1912 and Hall i'th Wood Folk Museum, the home of Samuel Crompton, inventor of the spinning 'mule', was also equipped and given by him. Lever Park and D'arcy Lever Park were other donations along with a number of paintings and works of art to form the nucleus of collections at several public galleries.

His one partial failure was on Lewis in the Hebridean Group of Islands off the West Coast of Scotland which he bought in 1915. Efforts to increase the material prosperity of the inhabitants by helping them to develop local crafts and improve the fishing industry met with considerable opposition from the crofters. Lord Leverhulme was finally forced to abandon his plans there during 1923 giving away 'Lews Castle' which had been his home.

Portrait of Lady Lever by Mrs. Maud Hall Neale.

He enjoyed better success on the Island of Harris, in the same group, where the islanders responded to his schemes for improvement and the port and town of 'Leverburgh' commemorate his beneficial enterprise.

A very meaningful existence resulted in recognition not only from Great Britain but from other countries to where Lord Leverhulme's soap combine had spread. His principal title was bestowed during 1922, when he was created a Viscount and chose to be 'Viscount Leverhulme of the Western Isles'.

This brief account gives some idea of the type of individual who became Lord of Rivington Manor and who has left such a fine legacy for so many to enjoy.

Lord Leverhulme's Coat of Arms.

Promotional advert issued by the manufacturer's of 'Roynton Cottage'. The illustration is misleading because it gives the impression that the building was sited much lower down the hill.

'Roynton Cottage' shortly after erection. Work on the gardens had not commenced at this stage.

Chapter 4 - The First Bungalow 'Roynton Cottage'

Being precluded from occupying Rivington Hall, having agreed to its rental to the Crompton family, Lord Leverhulme immediately put in hand the plans which he had for the construction of an alternative residence. His choice of dwelling was a little uncharacteristic, considering the almost palatial properties which he owned in other areas, a sectional wooden building which he entitled 'Roynton Cottage'.

The Portable Building Company of 46a Market Street, Manchester were responsible for the design and construction of the first bungalow the sections of which were, most probably, delivered by rail to Horwich Station and then transported to the site by horse and cart.

As previously discussed the site chosen, on the 1,000 ft. contour of Rivington Moor, seemed totally inappropriate but may have been due to an affection which Lord Leverhulme had for the spot. The type of building has also been the subject of some debate and two reasons have been advanced to show that it was only intended as a 'stop gap' measure. Firstly the pitch pine and red tiled roof 'hunting lodge' was assembled to offer Lord Leverhulme a base on the site quickly so that he could personally supervise development; and secondly that he eventually intended to replace it with a more permanent and substantial dwelling in another part of the grounds, when things had become established.

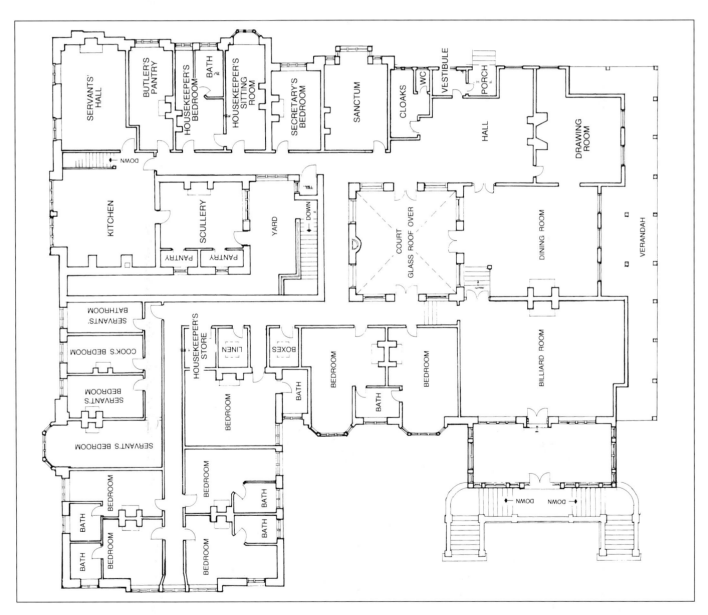

THE FIRST BUNGALOW - ROYNTON COTTAGE

Workmen on the site of Roynton Cottage. Circa 1900.

The sun-dial on the Orchestra Lawn, c.1905.

'Roynton Cottage' was nevertheless destined to remain, although the original square shaped structure with its westerly facing aspect was to be altered and extended out of all recognition; chiefly due to Lord Leverhulme's penchant for architecture.

A walled garden or 'garth' was constructed which adjoined the east side and was surrounded by 'Pergolas' (covered walkways formed of growing plants trained over trellis work). A circular stone dovecote was erected in the centre of the 'garth' with a bird bath at its base.

All modern conveniences were installed and the house was superbly furnished, its walls hung with tapestries, samplers., pen and ink drawings and family portraits.

'Black a'Moors Head public house known locally as 'The Black Lad'. It was demolished in 1903.

The ground floor was almost doubled in area and a second storey was added transforming the 'hunting lodge' into that "More permanent and substantial dwelling", and thus removing the need to build a replacement. The cottage was fit to entertain royalty and Lord Leverhulme was proud to invite his many influential and famous acquaintances to share his hospitality at 'Roynton Cottage'.

The tenant farmers on the Estate were not forgotten by the new landlord. On Saturday 9th January 1901, he presided at a dinner organised to allow them the opportunity of meeting him. All the farmers, their wives or eldest son/daughter were invited and some 80 of their number responded.

The guests were wined and dine in excellent style at the Black a'Moors Head public house, which was situated near to where Rivington Village Club now stands. They were entertained by a ventriloquist, a conjurer and a cinematograph exhibition was also given by Mr. Morris of Bolton.

As a point of interest the Black a'Moors Head was demolished in 1903 following persistent complaints from the Liverpool Water Authority that the inadequate provision of sewage disposal facilities was resulting in pollution of the reservoir.

Several events were in progress at one and the same time, the improvements to 'Roynton Cottage', the laying of the bungalow grounds, the setting up of a system of roadways throughout the Estate which connected with the existing transport routes and the gift of Lever Park.

THE BUNGALOW, RIVINGTON.

Nº 3.A.

'Roynton Cottage'. View across the lawn at the north front showing a gardener at work. (Circa 1906).

Royton Cottage. Circa 1905.

THE BUNGALOW RIVINGTON.   8.   THE BOWLING GREEN.

'Roynton Cottage'. A bowls game is in progress on the lawn. (Circa 1907).

I have already referred to the improvements taking place to the bungalow and will discuss the grounds and roadways later but the gift of 'Lever Park' is a complicated subject which I shall now endeavour to explain.

Rivington Hall Estate comprised 2,100 acres and it was Lord Leverhulme's intention to dedicate approximately 400 of those acres as a public park for the benefit of the townspeople of Bolton and the surrounding district.

His generous gesture was contained in a letter reproduced below:-

---

J. Simpson Esq.   Thornton Manor
F. W. Thompson Esq. and   Thornton Hough
Messrs Hulton, Son & Harwood, Bolton   Cheshire

6th September 1901

Dear Sirs,

I shall be obliged if you will communicate to the Mayor of Bolton on my behalf an offer to give to the Town of Bolton a portion of the lands in the parish of Rivington belonging to myself, which are enclosed within the undermentioned boundaries and more clearly shown on accompanying plan, to be used as a Public Park for the use and enjoyment of the Public for ever, but subject to the understanding that during my lifetime I may, provided same be done at my own sole expense, erect on such land any building or buildings for the use of the Public, or make any roads or footpaths thereon for the proper opening up of the land for the use of the Public and generally deal with the land as may appear to me to be desirable for the purpose for which the Park is intended, viz. its free and uninterrupted enjoyment by the Public.

BOUNDARIES:– A line drawn from the Black Lad in Rivington up Sheep House Lane, down Hall Lane, up the north side of Hall Wood to Old Kate's following the south east side of Hall Wood to the contour line at 600′ above sea level as shewn on the ordnance map, following approximately the 600′ contour line to the Douglas Brook in Shaw's Clough and then following the Douglas brook until the same reaches the Rivington Reservoir.

Within these boundaries there are other properties which do not belong to myself, and which of course are not included with the lands I am now proposing to give.

I also offer on the same conditions Rivington Pike, within the following boundaries:– On the north and north east side within the contour line at 1150′ above sea level; on the south and south west side within the contour line at 1125′ above sea level; and also sufficient land along the line of the two footpaths leading from the high road to the Pike, and measuring from the centre of said footpaths 60′ on each side, to make each of these approaches 120′ wide.

It will necessarily take some time before the land can be dedicated to the use of the Public, and in bringing this about I particularly wish that every consideration be given to the farmers and others who are tenants upon the estate, and that every reasonable care be taken to cause the minimum inconvenience.

If the Town of Bolton is pleased to accept this offer, I shall be obliged if you will take the necessary steps to have the property transferred, so that the matter may be completed on my return home in December next.

Yours faithfully,

W. H. Lever

In September 1901, Lord Leverhulme left England on a voyage to Australia, but a few days before sailing he arranged that during his absence representatives should convey his offer of the park to Bolton Corporation.

Lord Leverhulme's offer was gratefully accepted on behalf of the people of Bolton and the way seemed clear for things to progress on all fronts but storm clouds were gathering on the horizon to thwart the advance.

Liverpool Corporation Water Authority had the opportunity to buy Rivington Hall Estate before Lord Leverhulme became interested and even after the latter had completed his negotiations with Crompton he gave the Corporation an option to purchase at the agreed price but they declared no interest in being landowners.

In the spring of 1902 Liverpool Corporation promoted a Bill before Parliament to obtain powers to acquire certain areas comprised in the Rivington watershed including the Estate which Lord Leverhulme had bought. The Bill became before a Select Committee of the House of Commons on the 1st May 1902 and the Corporation were granted a

PLAN OF
RIVINGTON WATERSHED AND RESERVOIRS.

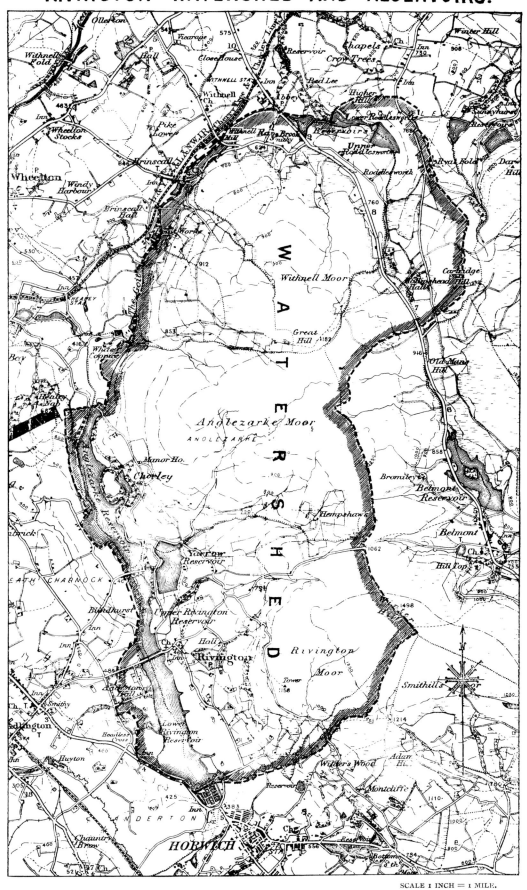

SCALE 1 INCH = 1 MILE.

compulsory purchase order for the lands with the exception of forty five acres which Lord Leverhulme could retain as the curtilage of his dwelling, with certain restrictions, and the proposed park was to remain as such and be known as 'Lever Park'.

The only question to be resolved was the price which Liverpool Water Authority should compensate Lord Leverhulme for his lands and wishing to avoid further expensive litigation the latter suggested that he be paid the purchase price of £60,000 plus his expenses to date. this was refused, and, as no mutually acceptable arbitrator could be agreed upon, an umpire was appointed by the Board of Trade.

Following investigation Lord Leverhulme was eventually awarded a sum which was almost double the amount he had paid for the whole Manor. In spite of an appeal by the Water Authority the judgement was upheld much to the chagrin of the Engineer-in-Chief whose opponent's name was to be perpetuated on lands belonging to Liverpool Corporation.

The uncertainty of the outcome of these proceedings meant that work was delayed to some extent but some progress had been made on both the bungalow grounds and the municipal park. Having covered the major developments to 'Roynton Cottage' it now remains to tell the story of its total destruction by fire.

'Roynton Cottage'. A second storey was added shortly before it was destroyed by fire - the familiar twin gables became a trio. (Circa 1912).

Lord and Lady Leverhulme can be seen standing behind the boys on the Great Lawn. (Circa 1907).

*Lord Leverhulme addressing boy scouts and members of the boys' brigade
from the Summer House on the Great Lawn.*

This post card view of Roynton Cottage was published by J. Geo. Davies, Photographer of Port Sunlight and was postally used in 1910. To the left of the bungalow can be seen the walled garden, or garth, and the dovecote is visible above the wall.

Roynton Cottage from the West Pergola, 1910.

Chapter 5 - Suffragist Outrage

1913 was a particularly unfortunate and sad year for Lord Leverhulme. He was then in his early sixties and might reasonably have been expected to be thinking in terms of easing the pace of his business life, by delegating responsibility to his subordinates and spending more time with his wife and son. This was not to be the case however because subsequent events robbed him of the opportunity as we shall see.

In the early part of this century women did not enjoy the status or liberty most do nowadays. There was no question of a female Prime Minister being elected or the "Sex Discrimination Act" reaching the statute books. The 'weaker sex' were subjugated in a male dominated society where they were considered merely as chattels. Protestations at the injustice of the situation were treated as something of a joke.

Tired of 'milk and water' approach to improving the lot of womankind a number of gifted and articulate females formed themselves into the Suffragette Movement, which was, in effect, an early form of the Women's Liberation Movement. The leading lights of the Society were Emmeline and Christabel Pankhurst who campaigned actively and vigorously for the right of women to vote in government elections. They even suffered terms of imprisonment in the fight for what they saw was their right.

Edith Rigby, wife of Doctor Charles Rigby of Winckley Square, Preston, was 40 years of age in 1913 and an active supporter of the Suffragette Movement. The life story of this very individual and determined lady in chronicled in an interesting publication entitled "My Aunt Edith", written by her niece, Phoebe Hesketh, a local authoress. Mrs Rigby had joined in many of the protest meetings and marches organised by the Suffragettes and had also served a number of terms of imprisonment for more militant activities. Imprisoned members of the cause continued to protest by going on hunger strike but a most

Edith Rigby of Winckley Square, Preston, who admitted the arson attack on 'Roynton Cottage'.

devious counter measure by government agencies caused much suffering amongst their number. The measure referred to was to confine the hunger striker until her health had deteriorated to a dangerous state and then release her. Following recuperation and convalescence outside prison, she was re-arrested to serve the remainder of her sentence. This was a most inhuman piece of legislation referred to as "The Cat and Mouse Act". The harsh treatment meted out to the Suffragettes resulted in a hardening of their resolve and indirectly led to the more serious manifestations of militancy.

Late on Saturday night, the 5th July 1913, there was a terrific explosion in a cafe underneath Liverpool Cotton Exchange. A piece of piping a foot long and an inch and a half in diameter was found to have contained explosive packed with stones and pieces of iron. No person was injured but considerable damage was caused to the Exchange. This incident is linked with the arson attack on Roynton Cottage, both acts of vandalism being later admitted by Edith Rigby.

Plans for the attack on the bungalow were carefully laid and executed as follows:

"Albert Yeadon, a resident of Preston, had been enlisted as an accomplice in the conspiracy to further draw attention to the plight of women. Yeadon's wife was allied to the Suffrage cause. Ironically, Edith Rigby needed the assistance of a strong man to carry the full paraffin containers to the site of Roynton Cottage.

About noon on Monday 7th July 1913, cans of paraffin were loaded into the boot of Doctor Rigby's motor car at Preston, and Edith Rigby, together with Albert Yeadon, were driven to Rivington by the family chauffeur. The latter was totally unaware of what was intended. On arrival at Rivington the paraffin was unloaded and the chauffeur was dismissed to await the return of his mistress and Mr Yeadon who then made their way to the bungalow grounds.

It had been ascertained, possibly by calling at one of the barns for refreshment, that no person would be in residence at Roynton Cottage on this particular day; which seems to confirm that there was no intention of causing death or injury to persons by the attack but strictly to cause damage to property. (It will also be remembered that no person was injured in the explosion at the Liverpool Cotton Exchange).

Having carried the paraffin to within easy reach of the bungalow, Edith Rigby said she wanted to complete the plan herself and asked Yeadon to leave and wait for her in the car. Edith walked around the bungalow checking that there was no one inside and started fires at several places by breaking windows and pouring paraffin through before igniting it with a taper. In the dry summer conditions the wooden bungalow was a veritable 'tinder box'. The fire soon took hold as Edith made her way back to the waiting transport.

The report in the Bolton Journal dated 8th July 1913, suggests that 'Roynton Cottage' was fired around midnight, which may or may not have been the case. A watchman connected with the Liverpool Waterworks first discovered the fire at about 1.30 am. on the 8th July and aroused Mr. Adamson, the residential engineer for the Waterworks, who lived in close proximity to the bungalow. He dressed quickly and on reaching the site saw the bungalow burning fiercely in three or four places on all sides of the building, the separate seats of the fire tending to suggest 'arson'. It was obvious, even at that stage, that Roynton Cottage was doomed, the pitch pine boards of the dwelling were well alight and night breezes were fanning the flames which raged out of all control.

Tenants of the lodges attached to the Estate were alerted and telephone calls were made to summon the Fire Brigade. Mr. Adamson spoke firstly with the Horwich (Lancashire and Yorkshire) Fire Brigade and later the Chorley Brigade were contacted but neither attended because Rivington was outside their recognised boundaries. Chief Officer Semple of the Horwich Brigade attended unofficially about 2.30 am. and directed the fire fighting efforts.

Alderman James Lawrence J.P. of Anderton Hall, which was situated directly across the Lower Rivington Reservoir from Roynton Cottage, saw the flames and telephoned the Fire Brigades at Horwich and Chorley. He could not contact the latter so he got out his motor car and drove there only to receive the same answer given to Adamson earlier. Realising the importance of informing Lord Leverhulme, Alderman Lawrence telephoned 'Thornton Manor', his Lordship's Cheshire home.

In July 1913 King George V and Queen Mary were making a Royal Tour of industrial Lancashire and spent the evening of Monday 7th July as guests of the Earl and Countess of Derby at Knowsley Hall. Sir William and Lady Lever were amongst the guests invited to dine with Their Majesties and left the Hall in the early hours of the morning.

It was 4.00 am. on the 8th July, when Alderman Lawrence contacted Thornton Manor. Whether Lord Leverhulme had then returned home or was still detained at Knowsley Hall is not clear but the information was eventually communicated to him and amongst the many expressions of sympathy which he received at the loss of his beautiful Rivington home was one from the King which read:-

"Much regret to learn from newspapers that while you were here last night (at Knowsley) your house at Rivington and its contents were destroyed by fire. I sympathise with you in your loss - George R.I.

The dreadful irony was that Lord Leverhulme was in favour of Women's Suffrage.

Several clues were left to indicate that the fire was the work of the Suffragettes. A small dispatch case left in the grounds contained a typewritten message which read:- "Lancashire's message to the King from the women, 'Votes for women due' - Message to the King, Liverpool: Wake up the Government. First give us reason to be loyal then try us".

The case also contained a pair of lady's grey suede gloves one of which was gashed across the palm and blood stained.

Edith Rigby pre-empted a successful enquiry when she gave herself up to the police in Liverpool on Thursday 10th July admitting both the explosives attack on Liverpool Cotton exchange and the arson outrage at Rivington. Insisting that she was solely responsible the explanation given for the Cotton Exchange attack was because of the grievance in that great cotton industry of Lancashire was built up on women's labour and whilst the merchants were willing to get power and wealth from that labour, women were denied the vote.

On being remanded in custody for these offences Edith Rigby made the following statement from the dock:-

"I want to ask Sir William Lever whether he thinks his property on Rivington Pike is more valuable as one of his superfluous homes occasionally to be opened to people, or as a beacon lighted for King and Country, to see that here are some intolerable grievances for women".

(Manchester Evening News 10th July 1913)

Although the loss of Roynton Cottage was a bitter blow, Lord Leverhulme determined to replace it with a more substantial residence and the second bungalow was thus planned to rise as a 'phoenix from the ashes'. It was to be constructed of stone and concrete giving little chance to the incendiary.

On the 19th July 1913 Lord Leverhulme left to inspect associated companies on the continent. Most unusually he travelled without his wife who had social engagements at home. Whilst in Marseilles he received a telegram informing that his wife was gravely ill and managed to reach her bedside just before she drifted into unconsciousness and died on the 24th July.

The remains of 'Roynton Cottage' following the arson attack.

Roynton Cottage from the 'Orchestra Lawn'.

This interesting post card view, taken from Lever Park, shows the skeletal remains of the burned out bungalow far left, with the lodge house and Rivington Pike also visible.

The burned out Bungalow from the Pike.

This shattering blow totally eclipsed the loss of 'Roynton Cottage'. Lord Leverhulme had first met his wife, then Elizabeth Hulme, when they attended the small private school in Wood Street, Bolton together as children. Their childhood friendship had blossomed into a deep and lasting love and they were married in 1874 being blessed with a son.

Following the death of his wife Lord Leverhulme paid this tribute to her:-

"It would be a poor compliment to my late wife if I left you with the impression she was a business woman, that she would make suggestions about the business, and suggestions about building the village and other institutions. She was essentially a womanly woman, and her knowledge of business was nil. But I always told her, as soon as I knew myself exactly how the business was progressing, and I can say, after full and careful thought, that I am convinced that without her influence there would have been neither a Port Sunlight, nor a Lever Brothers as we know it today. It came because of the confidence she inspired in me.

During the whole of our married life of forty years, however early business called me, I never breakfasted alone; she was always up and saw that the breakfast was properly prepared, and I always knew that whatever might happen during the course of the day the great event for her would be my homecoming in the evening.

Behind and before all our religion stands our home; Civilisation is founded upon the home; the centre of the home is the wife. A wife need not be an inspired genius in guiding and directing her husband. Genius might be a handicap and not a help - but she can be an inspiration and source of confidence the greatest inspiration to me had been the wife I was fortunate enough to win".

The loss of his closest companion had a deep and lasting effect upon Lord Leverhulme but he determined to overcome his grief by keeping it a personal matter and committing himself with renewed vigour to his multifarious activities.

As a memorial to his wife Lord Leverhulme erected the 'Lady Lever Art Gallery' in Port Sunlight Village. The building was opened on the 16th December 1922 by Princess Beatrice and remains an interesting place to visit.

Lady Lever Art Gallery

Three wooden 'pagodas' around the Japanese Lake were used as 'tea houses' on visiting days. Rice paper covered the windows as protection from the breezes and at night on these special occasions illumination was provided by copper lamps hanging from the 'pagodas', lamps in the stone ornaments and strings of electric light bulbs around the shores of the lake.

Chapter 6 - The Bungalow Grounds

Roynton Cottage existed for only a dozen or so years before it was destroyed by fire and I have covered the full sequence of events in the two preceding chapters in order to avoid confusion. It will be appreciated that the cottage, grounds and municipal park were developed in roughly the same time span and I will once again deal with events separately in order to afford the reader a clearer impression.

View of the Lancashire Plain across the Japanese Lake (foreground) and Lower Rivington Reservoir (middle distance). The replica of the ruins of Liverpool Castle is on the near shore (right) of the reservoir.

Looking across the boating lake towards the Loggia below the Pigeon Tower.

View across the 'orchestra' lawn. The sun dial - top left - was sited on a favourite picnic spot of Lord and Lady Leverhulme during their courtship. The photograph was most probably taken from the flat roof of 'The Bungalow'. (Circa 1925).

"In order to overcome the sloping angle of descent the gardens were laid out in terraces".

Harold Dickinson - haulier of Horwich - transporting stone for the construction of Rivington 'Dell'. The lead horse, named 'Nigger', was used on active service during the 1914 - 1918 war. (Photograph circa 1920).

Construction of waterfalls in the 'Dell'. The water course was diverted during building.

Below: Workmen in the 'Dell' - approximately 100 men were employed during construction - the foreman, (extreme right) was a cockney named Fletcher. (Circa 1920).

As can be seen by the bridge, this waterfall is the one shown under construction in the previous photograph.

A lower section of the series of falls through the 'Dell'. Note how the bridge design differs from the one in the previous illustration.

Close up view of a waterfall showing how successfully it was designed to appear as a 'natural' feature.

View of The Bungalow from the pathway which divides the Great Lawn. (Circa 1925).

Entrance to Japanese Gardens near to Stone House Lodge.

A very attractive view of the Japanese Lake taken shortly after its completion (Note the lack of vegetation). The stone ornament (centre) was cast in concrete and held a small lamp.

Japanese Lake from above - there was a habitat for water birds on the far bank.

Bridge and Lantern, Japanese Garden, Rivington Dell.

The Bungalow Grounds just below the Japanese Lake. Ernest Shone, the Estate Factor, can be seen to the right of the waterfall and below - left - are Rock Caves. (Circa 1920).

Below: The person standing in the pagoda gives some idea of how much rock was excavated to make the lake which was filled to a depth of 8 feet.

The Bungalow' from the Summerhouse
nearest the Pigeon Tower.

Dense rhododendrons presently obscure this view
of the Pigeon Tower from below.

The distinctive stone archway - right - is a
good reference point for this scene across
the Italian Gardens.

Having sited Roynton Cottage in such an isolated position the first priority was to establish lines of communication by road. This was achieved by widening and metalling existing moorland tracks and laying completely new stretches of road. Over twenty miles of roadway were eventually constructed which facilitated passage throughout the estate and connected with the routes from Horwich, Bolton, Chorley and Belmont. The following quotations from the book "Viscount Leverhulme" written by his son, embody Lord Leverhulme's attitude to road building -

"A friend, with whom he was walking one day along one of the many roads which he constructed at Rivington, asked him why he so fond of road-making. 'Well, for one thing', he replied, 'no one sees the ultimate usefulness of a road at the time I make it, and the result is no one thanks me for it. The road maker is the best anonymous servant of humanity".

He said on another occasion:-

"He drives a great broad thoroughfare from town to town, and for generations men travel over the road, with all their hopes and fears, with all their cares and joys, never once asking who it was that made their way easier for them. A road-maker's life is full of rich solitude and invisible rewards".

Thornton Manor
Thornton Hough
Cheshire

Dear Mr. Mawson

I am very pleased to have the opportunity of sending you my cheque for the remaining carved panel in the screen of your beautiful village church and wish you every success in your endeavours still further to improve its services.

Now that you have had the courage to ask me for a subscription, may I be so bold as to ask you to come and advise me upon the improvement of my garden at Thornton Manor? I have wanted to consult you for the last two years, but all of my friends warned me that it would be useless, as you never worked for anyone holding less social rank than a Duke, whereas I am only a poor and indigent soap-maker. Let me know if you can come, and when, naming two or three alternative dates.

Your faithfully
W. H. Lever

Following the assemblage of 'Roynton Cottage' work began on the grounds in earnest. The initial planning was carried out by local architects, most prominent among whom was Jonathan Simpson; Lord Leverhulme's life long friend from his school days in Wood Street, Bolton, he did not however make the most important contribution as we shall see.

Thomas Hayton Mawson was born at Scorton, a few miles south of Lancaster, on the 5th May 1861, making him almost ten years younger than Lord Leverhulme. Because Mawson was a delicate child his parents encouraged him to work in the gardens for both fresh air and in order to earn his pocket money. At 12 years of age Thomas went to Lancaster to work as an office boy and to learn drawing, building and horticulture. After two years of study he returned to employment with his father in newly secured property at Bentham; where the family eventually set up a nursery and fruit farm. These events decided Mawson on a career in landscape gardening in which he enjoyed enormous success.

Lord Leverhulme's meeting with T. H. Mawson was brought about, purely by coincidence, during the latter's attempt to obtain settlement of a debt. Mawson had designed a carved folding screen for a small church in Hest Bank and some part of the commission for the screen had not been paid. As Lord Leverhulme was regarded as a 'High Church Non-Conformist' Mawson wrote to him for a donation, enclosing a copy of the screen design. His Lordship was so impressed that he forwarded a sum of money and made the following request in his reply letter to Mawson;

After this first meeting during 1905 Mawson was extremely impressed with Lord Leverhulme and described him as a "veritable Napoleon in his grasp of all factors dominating any problem to be tackled". He referred to Lady Leverhulme as being "charmingly hospitable and careful for the comfort of her guests and always shed the radiance of a truly gracious spirit over the household". Lord Leverhulme was equally affected with Mawson's qualities and was pleased to commission him for work on both the "Bungalow Grounds" and "Lever Park".

Lord Leverhulme had already drawn the plans for a proposed layout of the bungalow grounds; as an amateur he said of himself; but Mawson said that they were truly remarkable. The estate was a planners dream affording vast scope for individual expression and the 'frames of reference' supplied to Mawson were that the gardens should be "laid out in perfect keeping with their natural environment".

An excellent working relationship developed between Lever and Mawson; because the former never showed surprise or disinclination towards imaginative schemes proposed by the artist. The challenge of establishing garden areas on the barren, windswept moorland was seized upon by Mawson; the chief reason being that all his professional counterparts prophesied failure and laughed at the notion of anything other than the hardy moorland grasses growing there.

Experiments were carried out to find what types of flora the covering soil of the hillside would support. Nurseries eventually flourished with many varieties of rhododendron and peat loving shrubs, together with a host of other hardy trees and plants. The results far exceeded Mawson's expectations and fully justified the confidence which he had initially felt at the success of this venture.

The bedrock of Rivington Moor is sandstone which has an unusual horizontal stratification. This feature inspired the design work for many of the garden structures and proved to be as advantageous in the construction of the grounds as it had initially been envisaged preventative.

The situation of 'Roynton Cottage' prompted the need for shelter which was provided by means of the pergolas and garth, mentioned earlier, along with a host of little shelters, fitted with seating wherever possible; loggia and summerhouses.

In order to overcome the sloping angle of descent the gardens were laid out in terraces, crossed by wide, crazy paved walkways; and the various levels were connected by stone flights of steps.

Throughout his life Lord Leverhulme enjoyed taking exercise whether it was swimming, walking, horse riding or a work out in the gymnasium. For him a garden was not a place to 'stand and stare' but for brisk promenading hence the long sections of walkway. The pergolas incidentally were constructed to form two L's (Initials of Lord Leverhulme) and were specifically to allow him to complete walking exercises during inclement weather.

Rivington Pike from the Western Shore of the Japanese Lake.

The grounds are divided into two sections by the roadway which runs from Sheephouse Lane, under 'Lord Leverhulme's Bridge' and connects with 'Old Will's Lane'., behind Rivington and Blackrod High School.

The upper section contained 'Roynton Cottage', the pigeon tower and loggia, a number of lakes, a series of miniature waterfalls, the lawns, shrubberies and Japanese Gardens. The lower section is largely wooded with waterfalls cascading through it. Four pathways run horizontally across this section at different levels which include bridges spanning the chasm of the largest waterfall from the Japanese Lake. A flight of 365 steps gives access through the lower gardens, which number signifies the days in a year as the four pathways are meant to represent the four seasons.

The lawn at the north front of Roynton Cottage is reputed to have been turfed from 'springy' grasses brought from Scotland. In the corner farthest from the house was situated a sundial which recorded the time accurately enough to be reliable. On the dial was a plate inscribed 'LIVE TODAY, NOT REGRETTING YESTERDAY NOR FEARING TOMORROW'. Diagonally opposite the sundial was a flight of semi-circular 'orchestra' steps connecting with the bungalow. On a fine evening the musicians played on the steps whilst guests used the lawn for dancing. Games of bowls, tennis, and croquet were also played there.

Terracing ran along the verandah at the west front of the house and a large telescope, mounted on a stand, stood on the terrace. On a clear day it was possible, with the aid of this telescope, to see as far south as the Welsh Mountains and as far north as the Lake District Hills. The names of places visible were engraved on the mounting for the telescope.

A range of greenhouses including a lean to fernery extended behind Stone-House Lodge. These were heated and the produce grown there amply supplied the bungalow kitchen with fresh vegetables. At the far end of the hot houses was a 'bothy' or small cottage, used by gardeners for potting plants, storage of implements, warmth, shelter etc.

A remarkable feat of excavation resulted in the construction of the great lawn situated about one hundred feet below the site of Roynton Cottage. This lawn is divided into two unequal parts by a crazy paved walkway which itself splits and runs along the top edge of each lawn. In addition to a number of small shelters there was a summerhouse adjacent to the pathway, in each part of the lawn. I am indebted to the staff at the Information Centre at Port Sunlight for allowing me to copy a number of photographs. Two of these particularly pleased me; one which shows Lord Leverhulme addressing a group of Boy Scouts and Boys Brigade members from a summerhouse, and the second depicting him on the lawn standing with these boys and their supervisors.

Gardeners at work in the Bungalow Grounds.

View along the walkway below the Four Gables Pigeon Tower. (Circa 1915).

In the largest section of the great lawn, some 325 yards long, a portion of the underlying rock was left at its natural level and clearly shows the enormous tonnage of material which must have been removed during the making. This chunk of rock stands almost seven feet above the grass level.

Lord Leverhulme's business ventures entailed a number of trips around the world and he was often influenced by what he saw on his travels. His gardens bespoke architectural features of Italian and Japanese extraction.

There are two series of waterfalls in the grounds the designs of which were derived from the hydraulic engineering feats associated with Italian formal cascades.

A 'miniature' series of waterfalls rise near the pigeon tower and fall into a small lake on each terrace. The first expanse of water in this line of descent is a lily-pond with a stone plinth in the centre on which there once stood a white stone statue of a boy standing on dolphins and blowing a horn; which seems to be an elongated sea-shell. This statue is known as ' King Neptune' but does not appear to me to depict this particular sea god. The second lake which these falls plunge into is much larger and was used as a boating lake. Water birds also made their homes in the banks of this pool adding to the interest.

A small stream which meandered through a leafy dell divided the grounds into two, almost equal parts. This rill was temporarily diverted whilst the sandstone bedrock was quarried to form a second series of waterfalls. A natural effect was achieved by using the quarried stone for construction work; the result being so successful that it is difficult to distinguish between the natural sections and the man made. Two single arched stone bridges were thrown over the chasm of the waterfall to connect the two halves of the garden and because the original stream was of insufficient force to warrant the cascades which had been engineered, a number of feeder streams were also diverted to augment the flow.

What is now known as the 'large lake' in the Japanese Gardens was in fact a compensation reservoir for the waterfalls during dry weather conditions. The lake and waterfall employed 100 men in the building and railway lines were laid to assist in moving the vast quantities of rock. Further stone was brought from a nearby quarry using horse and cart transport which was verified by the haulier contracted to do some of this work; Harold Dickinson of Horwich, who kindly allowed me to copy photographs.

The Japanese Lake has a concrete base and can be filled to a depth of eight feet. It was possible to empty the waters of the lake in 30 minutes by means of a penstock which was opened by a wheel locked away in a wooden hut hidden amongst the shrubbery. This was only done on isolated occasions but the surging waters descending the cataracts below were a magnificent sight.

The Japanese gardens were laid following an idea from Lord Leverhulme inspired by the 'Willow Pattern Design' and later extensive personal research in Japan. this design was introduced into England by Thomas Turner of Caughley about 1780 and the following is the tale which has been built around it:-

This white stone statue of a boy and dolphins was known as 'King Neptune'. The easily recognisable plinth can still be seen.

Summerhouse below the Pigeon Tower.

Bridge over the waterfall in the lower part of Rivington Dell.

View of Lever Park looking across the parapet of Lord Leverhulme's Bridge.

"A wealthy mandarin had an only daughter named Li-chi, who fell in love with Chang, a young man living on the island shown, who had been her father's secretary. The father overheard them one day making vows of love under the orange-tree, and sternly forbade the unequal match; but the lovers contrived to elope, lay concealed for a while in the gardener's cottage and thence escaped in a boat to the island. The enraged mandarin pursued them with a whip, and would have beaten them to death had not the gods rewarded their fidelity by changing them both into turtle doves. And all this occurred when the willow begins to shed its leaves".

The lake was the focal point of these gardens containing small rocky islets on which were situated stone ornaments, others were dotted about elsewhere in the grounds. Three wooden pagodas were erected around the lake which during visiting days were used as tea houses and had their windows covered with rice paper shutters to keep the breezes at bay. At night copper lamps hanging from these pagodas were lit to give the gardens the appearance of 'fairy land'. A story exists that the stone pathways running through the Japanese Gardens convey a message to the initiated, at points where they turn or junction.

Archway in stepped walk. (Circa 1906).

Exotic flamingos, swans and wild ducks found a home on the lake and completed the overall impression intended of a Willow Pattern scene. One can almost imagine the enraged Mandarin chasing the lovers across a bridge in these gardens, the doves which abounded throughout the grounds in those early days would doubtless add to the illusion.

Standing on a bridge in the Japanese Gardens are Joseph Henry Shone and Margaret Shone, parents of Ernest Shone. (Circa 1930).

Just before Lord Leverhulme's death, excavation work started to convert part of the Great Lawn into a second lake to increase the head of water to the falls. The railway track (left) was built to facilitate movement of stone. (Circa 1925).

BUNGALOW GROUNDS , RIVINGTON .   NO 7

Italian Loggia as seen from the boating lake. Seating was provided both inside and on the observation plateau.

*Visitors on the garden steps.
(1922). Mr. and Mrs. Wood with
their son Osmund on a day out in
the Bungalow Grounds.*

Time for relaxation on the great lawn. (1922).

Caves and grottoes were 'erected' in the Dell by using a similar technique to that employed in building the cascades, i.e. by partial excavation and using the excavated material for construction work. It was intended to put bears in the caves but this idea never came to fruition.

The following anecdote shows how well Mawson had laid the gardens to blend in with their natural surroundings:-
"One day Lord Leverhulme was showing a friend round the gardens when the latter remarked, ' It
must have been a big task to cut that path through the little hill'. Lord Leverhulme smiled and explained that, as
a matter of fact he had made the path first and then built up the hills on either side of it".

The size of the bungalow grounds extending to over 45 acres, make it impossible to discuss each and every feature; but I feel sure that the illustrations included along with the written description are sufficient to convey the breathtaking beauty of these "Hanging Gardens of Rivington".

'Roynton Cottage' from the terrace below the 'Pigeon Tower' with Belmont Lodge far left. (Circa 1910).

Chapter 7 - Miscellany

I have deliberately omitted to mention a number of important features of the grounds in the previous chapter in order to afford them special mention and hopefully give the reader a clearer understanding.

Lodge Houses

Lord Leverhulme owned several properties, the three principal ones being "Thornton Manor", Thornton Hough, Cheshire, "The Hill" at Hampstead, London, and "The Bungalow", Rivington, Lancashire. The situation of Port Sunlight in Cheshire and the fact that London, being the capital city, was the centre for business and commerce, meant that he had greater occasion to occupy the two former homes. 'The Bungalow' was more of a pleasant country retreat for him although he held a special affection for the place.

Absences from his property in Rivington for such long periods prompted the need for resident staff who could maintain the estate and provide security for the many valuable art treasures kept there. In 1906 Mawson was asked to construct gatehouses at 'Roynton Cottage' as well as the "pigeon tower". Bolton, Belmont and South Lodges were built of double weather board walling with thatched roofing. They were sited at the respective entrance points to the bungalow grounds and each comprised: sitting room, kitchen, scullery, pantry, bathroom, toilet and two bedrooms. It seems that South Lodge, situated at the entrance from Rivington Lane, was the "Cinderella" of the three because it was not fitted with either central heating or electric lighting, but was nevertheless a very comfortable and spacious abode. Stone House Lodge was built about 1915 and was of unusual design in that the entrance drive ran right through the centre of it. As the name implies it was stone built with a slate roof and consisted of sitting room, kitchen, scullery, pantry, bathroom, toilet, three bedrooms and two cellars.

The estate's main employees occupied the lodge houses and I was able to speak to Keith Shone who lived at Stone House Lodge, his father being employed as the 'Estate Factor'; and Jack Kings who moved into South Lodge with his parents in May 1926 when his father secured employment as a gardener on the estate.

Lever's Bridge

A popular feature of the grounds is Lever's Bridge which spans the road leading from Chorley to Horwich. Mr. Kings recounted a story that Lord Leverhulme asked his chief stone-mason, Edward Hart, to build a bridge over the road incorporating seven separate arches. Not fully understanding what his employer meant, Mr. Hart commented that the road was too narrow to be spanned by more than one arch, whereupon he was instructed to pack a suitcase for a journey on the following day. On joining His Lordship, as asked, Hart found himself on an Imperial Airways flight bound for Nigeria. On arrival he was shown a bridge which spanned a narrow gorge and was told to copy the design for the one intended at Rivington.

Stone House Lodge was built about 1915 and was of unusual design in that the entrance drive ran right through the centre of it.

South Lodge - The 'Cinderella' of the four lodge houses, being without central heating or electricity.

Lord Leverhulme with visitors to 'Roynton Cottage' circa 1906. (Belmont Lodge stands in the background).

The architectural details of the 'Romanesque' style bridge are purely attributable to Lord Leverhulme, who knew exactly what he wanted; and I can think of no finer way of conveying his wishes than by showing his workmen the actual design to be copied, albeit an expensive 'visual aid' to construction.

It had long been Lord Leverhulme's intention to erect a bridge in the grounds and he had completed a number of designs for the structure prior to the bridge being built. It was always a matter of great sadness him that his original sketches for the bridge were lost in the arson attack on 'Roynton Cottage'.

(My wife's grandfather, Paul Fairclough, was a stone-mason and worked on building projects in the bungalow grounds walking to the site from his home in Babylon Lane, Anderton.)

The Motor Car

Since 1885 when the two German engineers, Karl Benz and Gottlieb Daimler, independently produced vehicles powered by an internal combustion engine, with petrol as fuel, the development of the motor car has been very rapid. Early vehicles were slow, open to the weather, and gave a bumpy ride due to the tyres being solid.

Lord Leverhulme was an early user of the motor car and owned quite a number of vehicles. On long journeys he often took two cars so that he could stop from time to time to transfer into his own vehicle one of a group of people travelling in the second car, all of whom he wished to interview on various matters. This allowed him to utilise fully every minute of his time and it is true to the principles and tenets of Samuel Smiles.

The excellent roadways which Lord Leverhulme had constructed made Rivington a popular venue for motor trials and vehicles often took part in hill climbing competitions along the estate roads.

Stables, Garages and Power Plant

At the north east corner of the bungalow grounds, almost opposite the pigeon tower, there is a recess cut into the hillside which has the appearance of a disused quarry. This area is presently used as a sheep pen but it once contained the stabling and garage accommodation and the generating plant for Roynton Cottage.

With the rise in popularity and use of the motor vehicle some of the stabling was converted to house motor transport. Eventually there were two stone built heated garages sufficient to accommodate four vehicles. One of the garages was fitted with an Inspection Pit. There was also a detached petrol store built nearby.

Lord Leverhulme always had a passion for horse riding and became a familiar figure on his early morning rides through the leafy Rivington lanes. The stabling for his animals comprised a four stall stable with loft and a two stall stable. The stableman had a room provided above a harness store.

The electricity generating house was situated near to the garages and power was supplied by means of a 10 h.p. National Paraffin Engine.

Lord Leverhulme's seven arched 'Romanesque' style bridge.

Bolton Lodge from the Lower Drive leading to the front of 'The Bungalow'. The original thatched roof proved impractical and was replaced by tiles.

Lord Leverhulme on horseback visiting a scout camp at Rivington. (Circa 1907).

The roads leading to the Rivington Bungalow were improved to the extent where motor vehicles could use them.

Mr Cecil Edge in his Napier car after competing in a hill climb from Rivington Grammar School to a point near Rivington Pike, along the new road made by Mr W.H. Lever – later Lord Leverhulme. In those days motor trials were a frequent and popular feature at Rivington. (Photo 1907).

Keith Shone pictured near to Stone House Lodge. A motor car is parked next to him.

Visit of Literary Society to Roynton Cottage, 1911.

General Amenities

A telephone system was installed at both Roynton Cottage and Belmont Lodge, the telephone number incidentally was Horwich 28 which I considered as a suitable title for the work at one stage.

The water supply was piped from a spring near Winter Hill and both hot and cold water were on tap at Roynton Cottage and the Lodge Houses. The water supply was heated by coke fired 'Robin Hood' boilers situated in the cellars and central heating was provided by radiators. Drainage for the property was by the 'Septic Tank Principle'.

Open Day - A band plays on top of the summer house near the Great Lawn and even though it is raining the ice cream seller manages to attract children. (Circa 1930).

Open Days

The bungalow grounds were essentially private property and metal fencing was erected around the perimeter. It was not until the summer of 1919 that the general public were allowed an 'open day' being charged a nominal sum for admission, the whole proceeds being donated to charity. Almost 4,000 visitors attended on this occasion, benefiting local charities to the amount of £77. 4s . 5d and this initial success resulted in the exercise being repeated over the next five years.

The public were allowed free and unrestricted access to Lever Park; the second major landscape commission which Lord Leverhulme entrusted to T. H. Mawson.

Open Day - Visitors on the Great Lawn. (Circa 1930).

Open Day - The summer house and loggia had observation plateaux where visitors could take advantage of the views.

Open Day - Visitors descending the steps from the Pergola onto the 'Orchestra' Lawn. The group right of centre is approaching the sun dial. (Circa 1930).

Mowing the great lawn 1922. The rock in the background was left to show how much material was removed for the construction of the lawn.

The great lawn below the Bungalow. The rocky outcrop is visible far left.

Mrs. Shone beside one of the lanterns in the grounds.

Ernest Shone the Estate Factor.

The completed waterfall in the Dell.

The Japanese Lake with the Pike Tower visible on the skyline.

Stone House Lodge is on the extreme left with a pagoda standing next to it.
The second pigeon tower can be seen top right.

Geo. F. Smethurst, Photographer of 49 Chorley New Road, Horwich, took this
interesting shot of the 'bear caves'.

Visitors on the great lawn during 'Open Day' in the 1920's.

Lever Park near to Rivington and Blackrod Grammar School (left) - Lever Park Avenue had not been constructed at this time.

Lever Park near to Rivington and Blackrod Grammar School (left) - Lever Park Avenue had not been constructed at this time.

Chapter 8 - Lever Park and Rivington Estate

I have already explained a number of the steps leading to the development of Lever Park but I feel it prudent to recapitulate in order to give continuity.

Rivington Hall Estate extended over 2,100 acres and Lord Leverhulme offered 400 of these acres free to Bolton Corporation, for use as a municipal park, in September 1901.

Liverpool Corporation, most probably alarmed at this proposal, promoted a Bill to secure certain lands on the Rivington 'water shed' including Lord Leverhulme's Estate. Litigation ensued which resulted in the Water Authority being granted power to acquire lands in the Rivington drainage area with the exception of 45 acres which Lord Leverhulme was allowed to retain for his bungalow and grounds. The proposed plans for a 400 acre public park were upheld and it was to be named 'Lever Park'. Liverpool Corporation obtained free possession of this particular land because it was a 'gift' but were to permit Lord Leverhulme, at his own expense, to lay out the area for the use and enjoyment of the inhabitants of the County Borough of Bolton and generally of the public for ever.

Arbitration followed respecting the amount of compensation to be paid for those lands compulsorily purchased which resulted in the Water Authority being ordered to pay almost double the price which Lord Leverhulme had initially obtained the whole estate for.

These proceedings were not finally resolved until May 1905 although the first judgement was made during May 1902.

Following the acceptance of the gift of 'Lever Park' work began on its conversion for such use in June 1902. The object was to make the park "as free, as accessible and as attractive to the townsmen of Bolton and the public in general, as possible".

Suitable access was provided by roads, the next question being shelter for the thousands of visitors. This problem was solved with two immense Saxon tithe barns, Rivington Hall Barn and Great House Barn. Jonathan Simpson, Lord Leverhulme's local architect, was contracted to restore them for use and succeeded in putting the two structures into a thorough state of repair by reconstructing them in keeping with their original beam rafters and stonework. Kitchens were provided where large numbers of the public could be served with refreshments at moderate prices.

The Crompton family left Rivington Hall and moved to Cheshire following the death of John W. Crompton. This mansion of former squires of the estate was converted into a Picture Gallery and Art Museum and opened to the public free of charge.

BUNGALOW AND PARK, RIVINGTON.

'The Bungalow' from Lever Park - South Lodge can be seen bottom left.
The Pigeon Tower is top left and Belmont Lodge is top centre.

Plan
OF
THE BUNGALOW,
RIVINGTON,
LANCASHIRE.

For Sale by Auction by
Messrs. KNIGHT, FRANK & RUTLEY,
1925

To Chorley

To Belmont.

Old Kate's Close

Old Level (Coal)

Hall Wood

Rivington Hall Barn

Nursery

A Tank

Rivington Hall

Pigeon Tower

South Lodge

Belmont Lodge

VER PARK

Bridge

Liverpool Corporation

Breres' Meadow Pit

Breres' Meadow

THE BUNGALOW

Terraced Gardens

Liverpool Corporation

Stone House

Bolton Lodge

Ainsworths

Spring

Japanese Garden

Rivington Pike

Top o' th' Hill Farm

Spring

Liverpool Corporation

Spring

Tollorwich & Bolton

Brown Hill

Ward Hill

Old Quarry

Gilcbrook

Rising

Spring

From Horwich & Bolton

NOTE.—This Plan is published for the purpose of
indicating the position of the Property, and
although believed to be correct, its accuracy
is not guaranteed, and it shall not be
deemed to form part of the Contract.

Scale of Chains.

Links 100 0 1 2 3 4 5   10   20   30   40 Chains

NOTE—This Plan is based upon the Ordnance
Survey Map with the sanction of the Con-
troller of His Majesty's Stationery Office.

Martin Hood & Larkin Photoliths, Gt. Newport St. W.C.

Messrs. KNIGHT, FRANK & RUTLEY,
Auctioneers and Estate Agents,
20 HANOVER SQUARE, LONDON. W. 1
90 PRINCES STREET, EDINBURGH;
78 ST. VINCENT STREET, GLASGOW and
41 BANK STREET, ASHFORD, KENT.

Exterior view of Great House Barn.

Gt. House Barn. Rivington. C. Cross.

Interior view of Great House Barn.

Ethel Coupe (nee Mulligan) with her dog Scruff outside Great House Barn. Circa 1938.

Interior of Rivington Hall Barn.

Rivington Hall Barn shortly after it was renovated. (Circa 1904).

PLAN OF TABLES FOR THE OPENING OF LEVER PARK
MAY 18TH 1904

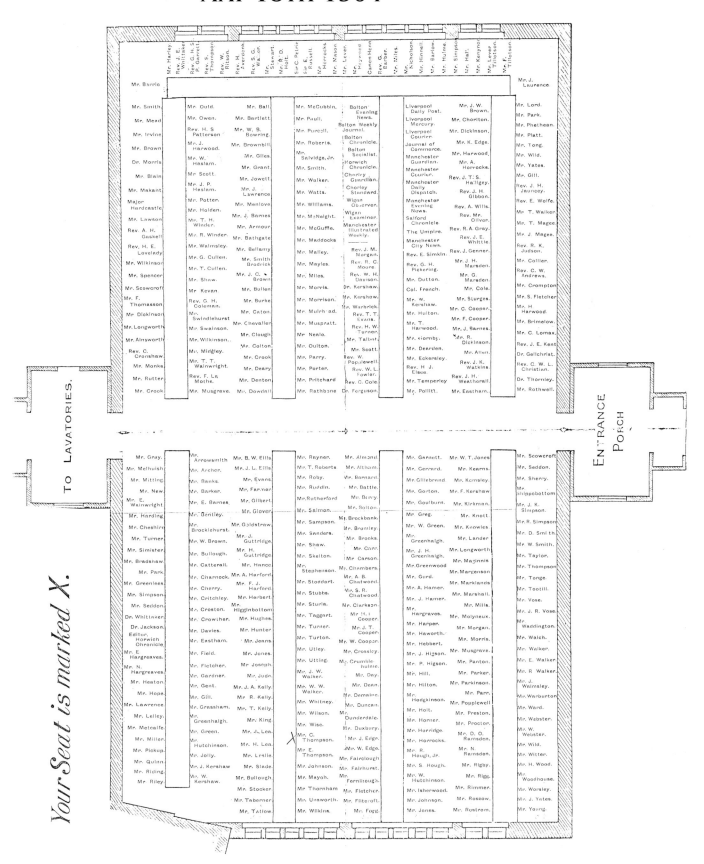

OLD BARN, LEVER PARK.

OPENING of
LEVER PARK, RIVINGTON,
By W. T. MASON, Esq., M.A.

LUNCHEON AT 1-30 P.M.

MENU.

JULIEN SOUP.

MAYONNAISE OF SALMON.   PRAWNS IN ASPIC.

ROAST CHICKEN.   CHICKEN A LA BECHAMEL.
YORK HAM.   OX TONGUE.
ROAST LAMB.   SPICED BRISKET BEEF.
POTATO SALAD.   ITALIAN SALAD.

FRUIT JELLY.   LIQUEUR JELLY.   MERINGUE CREAM.

CHEESE AND BISCUITS.

COFFEE   DESSERT.

Programme and letter of acceptance acknowledgement for the Opening Ceremony of Lever Park on Wednesday 18th May 1904.

THORNTON MANOR,
THORNTON HOUGH,
CHESHIRE.
May 16th, 1904.

DEAR SIR,

I am honoured by your acceptance of invitation for Luncheon at Rivington on Wednesday, and now advise you that conveyances have been arranged to leave the Town Hall, Victoria Square, at 11.45 a.m., to convey you and other guests to Rivington. The conveyances will travel by Deansgate, Marsden Road, St. George's Road, Chorley New Road, Horwich, Rivington Lane, etc.

It would facilitate the arrangements if you would present this note at the time of taking your seat in the vehicle.

Yours faithfully,

W. H. LEVER.

Beech House Rivington with 'Roynton Cottage' on the skyline.

*View of Lever Park
with Woods' Farm
(centre).*

*Closer view of
Woods' Farm.*

*Beech House from the
slopes of Rivington Moor.
Anderton Hall stands
opposite across the Lower
Rivington reservoir.*

91

Rivington Hall Farm.

Rivington & Blackrod Grammar School. (Circa 1906).

'The Clog'. Anglezarke. (now demolished).

Higher Derbyshires Farm, Lever Park, Rivington.

Knowle House, Rivington.

Sweetloves Farm. C.1903.

93

Summerfield, the one time home of Mr. Hinnel, Town Clerk of Bolton from 1865 to 1905.

Darbyshire's Cottage, where Mr. C.J. Darbyshire lived, who was Bolton's first Mayor in 1839.

Great House Farm from top o'th hill. In the bend of the road, to the right, where people can be seen, there was once a Ford.

Higher wards or Clock House Farm, last occupied by the Leigh Family and demolished in 1905.

Intack farm, which was built in 1712 and finally demolished in 1908.

Red Cot, which was built for Mary Susan Ainsworth about 1899. She was the sister of Arthur Walton Ainsworth of Beech House, Rivington.

Mill Hill Cottages, built by John Hampson in 1788.

Pall Mall Cottages are to the right with Beech Cottage behind the Telegraph Pole.

Rivington Village School c.1902. This was originally Rivington Grammar School founded by Bishop Pilkington in 1566.

Ward's Cottage, c.1905. This photograph shows the demolition of Ward's Farm.

Ward's Cottage, once part of Ward's Farm, was built by Thomas Brownlow in 1720, and is visible in the centre, Circa 1938.

Group of bystanders
admire a black swan
gliding across
Rivington Hall Lake
after it was divided.

Trees were planted beside the newly constructed roads, fields were fenced and a number of paddocks were erected stocked with deer, buffaloes, emus, yak and many other animals. A herd of Chartley cattle were introduced which are the original native breed of these Islands.

A small lake in front of Rivington Hall was divided into two by constructing a road through the centre of it which connected with Great House Barn. Black swans from Western Australia were introduced to the eastern section of the divided lake and white swans to the western half.

The whole impression was that of an 'open air zoo' and it is easy to imagine the delight and wonderment of visitors on seeing, most probably for the first time in their lives, such unusual animal and bird life. It was appreciated however that the chief interest was in the green fields and open spaces where people could wander at will, take 'al fresco' meals or merely 'sit and stare'.

Lever Park was opened on the 18th May 1904, when at 1.15 pm. on that day, W. T. Mason Esq., M.A., a former Headmaster of Bolton High School for Boys, formally conducted the ceremony outside the entrance to Rivington Hall Barn in front of a large and representative gathering. Four trees were planted to commemorate this event and luncheon followed in the Barn where entertainment was provided.

There was still much work to be done on the park and the commission was granted to T. H. Mawson, as discussed previously, following his meeting with Lord Leverhulme in 1905.

Mr. Winstanley, assistant keeper, with a lioness cub in Lever Park.

Zebras in 'Lever Park'.

Liverpool Corporation was consulted at every stage by Lord Leverhulme's representatives and voiced no opposition to his plans. In retrospect there is no reason why the issue could not have been solved more amicably without invoking the acrimonious arbitration. There is little doubt that ignorance of the full facts meant that Lord Leverhulme's standing was far less in Liverpool than elsewhere which was a dreadful pity because he was forced into a situation against his will and reacted in a reasonable and rational way.

The following quotation from the work of "Lord Leverhulme" by W. P. Jolly hints at a possible explanation:-

"It is remarkable how often Lever seems to bring out the worst in public officials. Sometimes it almost seemed that they resented the way he achieved instant reforms by spending his own money, when they were struggling to do much the same using public funds".

Presentation to Rev. W. Ritson, Vicar of Rivington Church and Mrs. Ritson on their retirement in 1918. Lord Leverhulme is stood centre right of the group outside Rivington Hall Barn.

Rivington Chapel.
C.1905.

Rivington Church.
C.1905.

Interior of Rivington Church.

Liverpool Castle was the first nucleus of the City and was eventually demolished to make way for commercial development. As a final touch to Lever Park a replica of the ruins of Liverpool Castle were erected on a hillock known as "Coblowe", which is situated on the eastern side of the Lower Rivington Reservoir. Work was commenced on the ruins about 1912 but proceeded slowly employing only a handful of stonemasons and labourers. The plans were never finally completed and work ceased after Lord Leverhulme's death. The ruins were a bold experiment in landscape design and the result, after the newness of the stonework had worn away and become covered with moss and lichen, was eminently successful.

Lever Park was virtually completed in 1911 and with all due ceremony the Park was officially dedicated for use by the public on the 10th October that year. The workforce and villagers celebrated with a luncheon and dance in Rivington Hall Barn whilst the main guests enjoyed their own luncheon and speechmaking in Rivington Hall.

The principal features of Lever Park are as popular today as ever they were. Rivington Hall and the two Barns still host social functions and refreshments are available at the Barns during weekdays. A small aviary exists near to Rivington Hall stocked with a variety of birds but the animals have long since departed. The replica ruins of Liverpool Castle remain an enigma to those unaware of their history. The effects of nature have so mellowed the structure that it appears as a totally authentic ruin which was what the builder intended.

Aerial view of the replica of the ruins of Liverpool Castle built on 'Coblowe' by the eastern shore of Lower Rivington Reservoir.

Liverpool Castle

Chapter 9 - The Second Bungalow

There is always some good to come out of evil even if it is only the knowledge of how and why the tragedy occurred can assist us to avoid or prevent a repetition in the future. The fact that Roynton Cottage was a timbered dwelling exacerbated the losses incurred and so Lord Leverhulme determined that the replacement would be structured of stone and reinforced concrete which materials at least would be non-combustible.

Fortunately the first bungalow was covered by insurance and the compensation monies would go some little way towards the cost of re-building. Two other aspects of the fire loss which could be considered beneficial were, firstly, that Roynton Cottage was not totally in keeping with the unique gardens which had been landscaped around it as they bespoke an even finer residence; and the opportunity was presented to build a magnificent replacement. Secondly, the devastation felt by Lord Leverhulme at the loss of his wife needed an outlet and the architectural challenge of designing the second bungalow was irresistible. It provided him with the opportunity to occupy his mind on positive ventures and thus lessen the pain of his inner grief.

Throughout his life Lord Leverhulme had a genuine love of architecture which was due to his interest in art. This was officially recognised in 1918 when he was appointed an Honorary Fellow of the Royal Institute of British Architects.

A friend said of him:-

"The love of the beautiful in art and nature has always been a strong feature in his judgement and   taste".
His son said of him:-

"Altering the face of nature was with him a passion. He was never happier than when seated in front of a plan with a drawing board, ruler and 'T' square ready to hand. Architecture was always an absorbing study for him, and one can safely say that no single man - at any rate in modern times - has ever built a larger number of houses and buildings and constructed a greater mileage of roads. With him it was never a case of leaving everything to the architect and settling the bill   when the work was finished. Expert advice he wisely sought and freely acknowledged, but the plan and lay-out of Port Sunlight were his own, and so, in the main, were the plans for the works and buildings in the village, and in many cases of the houses also. The architects he employed all looked upon him as unique amongst their clients. He did not employ them - he collaborated with them".

Lady Lever commented that she seldom experienced the sensation of living for very long in a house free from the presence of workmen.

In 'collaboration' with Lord Leverhulme, Jonathan Simpson designed a single storey replacement bungalow constructed of stone with random coursed walling in conformity with the ancient Lancashire traditions; the flat roof being of reinforced concrete giving little chance to the incendiary.

'Roynton Cottage' had a westerly facing aspect which left it open to the fiercest assaults of the prevailing winds and so 'The Bungalow' was sited facing south. Any intention which Lord Leverhulme may have had to re-position his dwelling was precluded once the grounds became so well established.

The garth and pergolas were incorporated as an integral part of 'The Bungalow'; which name Lord Leverhulme chose for his new home. It is difficult however to imagine a more inappropriate title because the planned dwelling was far removed from the popular conception of a bungalow being more in keeping with a 'country mansion'.

Little time was lost in rebuilding and within a year of 'Roynton Cottage' being burned to the ground, Lord Leverhulme was in residence at 'The Bungalow'. A date stone commemorating the completion in early 1914 was included over the main entrance to the house.

South front of 'The Bungalow' 1918, before the second storey was added. Note that the dovecote has not yet been sited on the grass island in front of the property.

In front of 'The Bungalow' where the driveways from Stone House Lodge and Bolton Lodge converge on the forecourt, an old stone sign post was sited which gave the residence an air of antiquity. An interesting story is attached to this stone which is known as the 'Headless Cross'. The monument has the legs of a man on one face of the supporting stone and other designs on the remaining three faces. The square stone on top has the four sides carved with directions to Wigan (spelt with two g's), Bolton, Preston and Blackburn (inscribed Blagburn).

Dovecote inside the walled garden or 'Garth'. This was removed to the front of 'The Bungalow' when the ballroom replaced the 'Garth' in 1922.

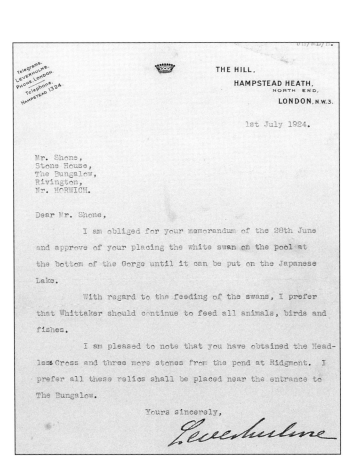

Lord Leverhulme was kept informed of developments at Rivington. This letter was received by the Estate Factor and verifies the story concerning the 'Headless Cross'.

Joseph Ridgway who built Ridgmont House in 1809 was a collector of stone monuments and following his death in 1842 the 'collection' was neglected and fell into disrepair. Lord Leverhulme had heard this story and asked Ernest Shone, the Estate Factor, to search the Ridgmont area for suitable stone. Shone located the 'Headless Cross' by means of grappling irons, on a flooded section of the lands and the Cross along with the base stones were recovered and sited in front of 'The Bungalow'. Following demolition the 'Headless Cross' was erected at its present position in Grimeford Village on the wide grass verge where Roscoe Lane Brow junctions with Grimeford Lane and Rivington Lane.

'The Bungalow' largely comprised the following accommodation:-

                    Outer and Inner Halls
                    Dining Room
                    Morning Room
                    Library
                    Study
                    Four Principal Bedrooms
                    Four Principal Bathrooms
                    Five Servants Bedrooms
                    Five Servants Bathrooms
                    Complete Domestic Offices

Inevitably it was altered on many occasions to suit Lord Leverhulme's complicated idea of perfection; approximately one hundred alterations and improvements were carried out up to the time of His Lordship's death in 1925. R. Hermon Crook F.S.A., Architect and Surveyor of 17 Mawdesley Street, Bolton, successor to Jonathan Simpson, was responsible for designing much of the architectural change to 'The Bungalow'. Specialist contracts were of course undertaken by appropriate firms, the name of Robert Walsh, Plumbing and Heating engineers appearing on plans for additions and alterations to the heating, and hot and cold water supplies, during 1920.

Winter Garden - west front.

Winter Garden - north front - entrances were situated between the fish tanks giving access to the Morning Room, Lord Leverhulme's Study and a Bedroom respectively.

Dining Room - The lamp shade was made from sea shells collected from the South Sea Islands and was extremely lightweight. A plan of the Constellations of the Northern Hemisphere was delineated on the panelled ceiling.

Pigeon Tower.

This corner building contained the Aviary.

Unglazed Pergola from the Cascade.

Pergola from the North Front.

The Ballroom and Orchestra Steps from the Lawn.

North Front from the Orchestra Lawn..

West Elevation of 'The Bungalow' and Small Pigeon Tower viewed from the Great Lawn.

Front of 'The Bungalow' with Dove Cote.

Both the main entrance and the servant's entrance were situated at the front of 'The Bungalow'. The beautiful solid oak doors were 'pegged' with wooden dowels and each door had two hinges at the top and bottom which 'wrapped' around the woodwork and were held in place by coach bolts.

'Upstairs' and 'Downstairs' quarters were in fact side by side at 'The Bungalow', the domestic section being entirely shut off from the main part of the house. All the main rooms were floored with polished oak or polished oak parquetry blocks, whilst the bathrooms, cloakrooms, secondary entrances and domestic offices had mosaic tiled covering. Italian craftsmen were contracted for the tiling and a special feature was that the edging tiles curved upwards where they joined the wall both to prevent dirt lodging and make cleaning easier.

Lord Leverhulme's bedroom measured 19 ft. by 13 ft. and was fitted with a marble hand washbasin and heated towel rail. The whole of one side of the room was glass panelled and opened onto the Winter Gardens as did all the principal rooms in the house. A bathroom, gymnasium and tea room completed the master's suite. It was Lord Leverhulme's custom to get up around 5.00 am. when he was in residence at 'The Bungalow' and due to his deafness a 'Klaxon Horn' fitted over his bed doubled as his alarm clock. The sound of this infernal instrument not only wakened him but also the resident staff, tenants of the Lodge Houses and half the population of Rivington and Horwich in the process. Once out of bed he had a cold bath and exercised on a mechanical horse which 'shook' him dry. Twenty minutes in the gymnasium, a cup of tea and then dealing with correspondence until 7.30 am. was the start of his 'Working Day'. It seems that one of the secrets of Lord Leverhulme's staying power was his ability to enjoy a short nap in the middle of the day.

Inner Hall with roof light. A fireplace alcove situated on the left where the tiger skin rug is visible.

Morning Room - The door to the right gives access to the Library.
The glass partition on the extreme right opened onto the Winter Gardens.

There was direct access from Lord Leverhulme's bedroom to the Study, the dimensions of which were 18 ft. 9 ins. by 12 ft. 8 ins. Leaving the Study along a short corridor one entered the Inner Hall measuring 45 ft. 6 ins. long by 21 ft. 4 ins. wide; the latter measurement included a deep recess which was fitted with an arched brick fireplace and tiled hearth.

Dimensions of the Morning Room which adjoined the Inner Hall, were 41 ft. 6 ins. by 19 ft. 9 ins., which included a bay. A second arched brick fireplace with tiled hearth was fitted there.

The Dining Room was most impressive, the four roof support pillars being covered in plaster to disguise their function with a touch of neo-classicism. The panelled ceiling was decorated in blue and relieved by stars arranged in a plan of the Constellation of the Northern Hemisphere. Exclusive of two entrance recesses, the room measured 36 ft. 10 ins. by 24 ft. 9 ins. and was fitted with a finely ornamented marble fireplace. The walls of the Lounge situated between the Dining Room and Winter Garden were hung with Japanese wicker.

A Library measured 19 ft. 6 ins. by 14 ft. 6 ins. and was fitted with bookcases the shelves of which were extremely well stocked. It had a polished oak floor and a pair of glazed doors led to the Winter Garden.

I was extremely pleased to obtain a ground floor plan of 'The Bungalow' which has made it much simpler to locate and explain the various rooms. By relating the plan to the text and illustrations included it is much easier to appreciate this well designed, functional and yet beautiful residence. The property was exceptionally well appointed with furnishings and art works of inestimable value. Lord Leverhulme's arrangement of pictures and furniture was unerringly precise and balanced but he had a tendency to overcrowd. It was said of him that he furnished his rooms to be looked at rather than lived in.

Household staff enjoyed a high standard of accommodation similar in most respects to the extremely comfortable principal guest rooms. The kitchen was centrally positioned for convenience of service and was fitted with a double oven 'Eagle' range. There was also a heated linen room, butler's pantry, scullery, store room, larder and even a servants' sitting room. A telephone extension connected the butler's pantry with Belmont Lodge. All the principal apartments had electric bells fitted communicating with the kitchen where an indicator board alerted the staff that their presence was required.

The pergolas extending along the north and west fronts of 'The Bungalow' were glazed and the crazy paved walkways were carpet covered for warmth. Wisteria, Honeysuckle, Clematis and other varieties of climbing plant overhung the walkways and a series of fish or lily pools, enclosed by a pretty rock-like stone with centre fountains, added further interest.

A spiral metal stairway gave access onto the flat roof of the dwelling which was fitted with sky-lights that had ventilation windows opening vertically thus allowing kitchen odours etc. to escape and preventing rain penetration.

The telescope which existed on the terrace of 'Roynton Cottage' was retained as a popular feature but was housed in a custom built observatory at 'The Bungalow'.

Apart from the Ballroom, which I will cover specifically in the following chapter, the latest addition to 'The Bungalow' was an apartment for the housekeeper built over the servants' entrance in the form of a second storey. It is thought that this functional suite had the dual purpose of shielding from view the dome of the ballroom when approaching from the south front.

The cessation of hostilities in the Great War, waged to end all wars, saw the country in a celebratory mood following years of strife and there was a re-awakening of interest in dancing and social activities in general. Always abreast of the times, if not ahead of them, Lord Leverhulme entered the 'Roaring Twenties' in fine style.

'The Bungalow from the 'orchestra' lawn. The dome of the ballroom ceiling is visible extreme left.

Chapter 10 - The Last Waltz

During 1920 Lord Leverhulme re-discovered the love of dancing which he had enjoyed in youth and early manhood. It held a threefold attraction for him firstly, as a form of exercise, secondly, as a means of entertaining visitors and thirdly, it allowed him to indulge in what was essentially a youthful and light hearted pastime. Being almost 70 years of age he was conscious of what his contemporaries might think of this new found form of recreation and on one occasion he asked his son for a candid opinion. The reply was to the effect that there could be no possible harm in amusing himself in this way and absolutely no reason why it should provoke adverse comment. Grateful for this reassurance Lord Leverhulme commented :-

> "Well the explanation is simply this: I spend the day entirely surrounded by men, and I don't want to spend my evenings also in ponderous conversation with men. I like to have a few young friends about me whom I can chaff. It keeps my mind young and prevents me from becoming dull and heavy".

The Ballroom was designed by R. Hermon Crook and replaced the 'garth' which was demolished to make way for it. The dovecote from the centre of the 'garth' was re-positioned on the forecourt of 'The Bungalow'.

Of circular design the ballroom was 44 ft. 6 ins in diameter and the oak parquetry block floor was specially sprung for dancing. (If necessary it could also be 'locked'). It can simply be described as a circle within a rectangle the latter being the area of the 'garth'. Of the four corners of the rectangle outside the circle's circumference, two were used as alcoves, one as a lounge and lavatories were situated in the one remaining.

A glass dome in the centre of the ceiling gave light whilst the rest was decorated in blue and dotted with gold stars which were arranged as the constellations appeared on the 19th September 1851, the date of Lord Leverhulme's birth. This design was prepared by R. Hermon Crook.

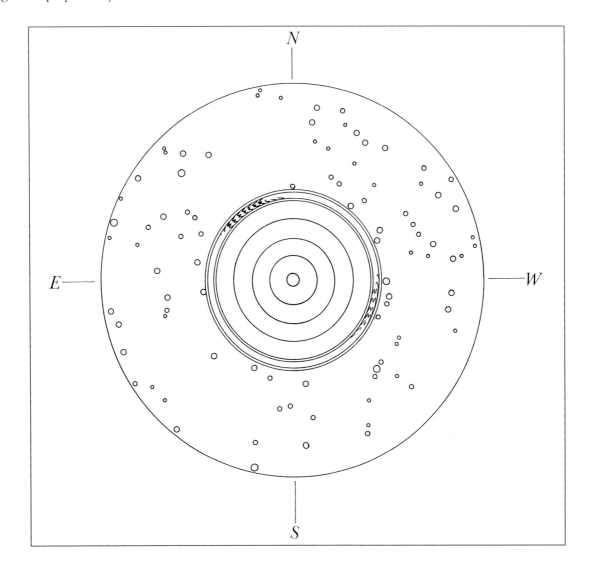

Interior of the Ballroom. The ceiling was blue with gold stars arranged as the constellations appeared on the 19th September 1851, the date of Lord Leverhulme's birth.

Programme for a social function at Rivington Hall Barn.

Portrait of Lord Leverhulme by artist, Augustus John.

Miniature fluted pillars supported the two fireside alcoves and they were fitted with finely carved oak mantels and jambs one of which came from the Island of Lewis. Keith Shone recollected that the latter mantel existed in a public house on Lewis and for generations local families had carved a section apportioned to them. Lord Leverhulme tried to buy the fireplace but without success but eventually purchased the whole building just to obtain this desirable artefact.

Inside views of the ballroom included, convey much more of the exquisite furnishings than mere words. The beautifully carved gilt wood framed wall mirrors each side of the doorways and the intricate ornamentation above add interest. A pair of early Italian gates 3 ft. high by 6 ft. 6 ins. wide were positioned above the exit to the buffet / lounge and during 1923 a minstrels' gallery was built over the vestibule. A grill partially hid the musicians but the placement of the gallery meant that the dance floor was not obstructed.

Hung on the wall of the ballroom was a Flemish panel of unusually large dimensions (33 ft. long by 9 ft. wide). During the sale of effects from the ballroom in 1925 this tapestry fetched £2,400, a considerable sum of money in those days. When not in use the ballroom floor was covered with a circular Persian carpet 19 ft. 6 ins. in diameter. This carpet was originally made in the harem of a Persian Prince and was bought from Lady Ratan Tata. The seating in the ballroom was provided by individual chairs arranged around the edge.

His Lordship's deafness must have been quite a handicap on the dance floor. Even though he was an accomplished 'lip-reader' people wondered how he could follow the music or hear the start of a dance tune. It is reported that he had a small blue light installed in the ballroom ceiling which would light up and reflect in his patent leather shoes at the appropriate times; obviously switched on by an 'accomplice'. This simple device saved him some embarrassment and demonstrates his ingenuity.

Speaking of embarrassment, an amusing story is told by Lord Leverhulme's son concerning a portrait which his father commissioned the celebrated Welsh artist, Augustus John, to paint in June 1920. When the work was finished at the end of August and despatched to His Lordship for approval he was less than flattered with the likeness of himself depicted on the canvas. Determined that no one should see the painting he immediately sent it for storage at 'The Bungalow', Rivington where it was his intention to hide it away in a safe. When Lord Leverhulme came to store away the offending painting in the safe, it proved too large so he cut out a square of the canvas which included the head and placed that in the safe. The remainder of the painting, together with the frame, were then placed into the packing case in which they had arrived.

Unfortunately his conscientious housekeeper noticing that the case was 'returnable' had it nailed up and forwarded to Augustus John. The artist was obvious surprised at receiving back his work in such a mutilated condition and contacted Lord Leverhulme. The latter explained, quite frankly, what had happened and apologised for the embarrassing error. Although a little annoyed Augustus John accepted the circumstances but the Press got wind of the incident and the ensuing publicity led to a one day strike of artists in support of Augustus John.

The staff employed at 'The Bungalow' were charged with a great responsibility because the master was absent so frequently and for such long periods. Trips around the world and time spent at his other homes meant that Lord Leverhulme only visited 'The Bungalow' intermittently for short stays.

During 1925, when 74 years of age, Lord Leverhulme undertook a trip to West Africa against the advice of his doctors. The trip affected his health and on his return friends noticed that he did not look well even though he continued with his public duties.

On 27th April 1925, he travelled from Rivington to his home in Hampstead and the following day he was confined to bed with an attack of bronchitis. Despite a slight improvement, pneumonia eventually developed and at 4.30 am. on Thursday 7th May 1925 Lord Leverhulme died peacefully at his London home.

Tributes poured in from all parts of the world but on a personal level the staff and workmen employed at 'The Bungalow' were thrown into a state of uncertainty at the loss of their employer. Executors were appointed to administer Lord Leverhulme's holding and it was eventually decided to sell Rivington Hall Estate. Approximately one hundred workmen who had been carrying out improvements on the house and gardens were laid off leaving only the domestic staff and two joiners. The animals in Lever Park were offered to Bolton Council free of charge on condition that they would be looked after but many were eventually given to Belle Vue Zoo in Manchester or destroyed, the cost of keeping them being too prohibitive.

Messrs Knight, Frank and Rutley of 20 Hanover Square, London, were directed by the executors of the late Viscount Leverhulme to auction 'The Bungalow' and contents as well as the contents of Rivington Hall. At 2.30 pm. on Thursday 5th November 1925, the auction of 'The Bungalow' took place at the Midland Hotel, Manchester, and the property was purchased by John Magee of Magee Marshall and Company, Brewers of Derby Street, Bolton, for £15,000. The contents of 'The Bungalow' and Rivington Hall were auctioned in situ on Monday to Friday 9th to 13th and Monday and Tuesday 16th and 17th November 1925, from 1 pm. each day and John Magee purchased approximately £10,000 worth of goods.

Newspaper report on Lord Leverhulme's Will - Daily Dispatch, Friday July 10th, 1925.

THE LEVERHULME COLLECTION
ORDER OF SALE

ORDER OF SALE.

At THE BUNGALOW.

FIRST DAY.—Monday, November 9th.

PICTURES, DRAWINGS AND PRINTS.   LOTS.
1— 192

SECOND DAY.—Tuesday, November 10th.

THE COLLECTION OF
NEEDLEWORK PICTURES,
TAPESTRIES, AND
OLD STAINED GLASS,   193— 395

THIRD DAY.—Wednesday, November 11th.

CHINESE AND EUROPEAN PORCELAIN,
Bronzes, and
OLD ENGLISH FURNITURE.   396— 596

FOURTH DAY.—Thursday, November 12th.

CANTON ENAMELS,
BEDROOM EQUIPMENT,
BALLROOM FURNITURE, ETC.   597— 777

FIFTH DAY.—Friday, November 13th.

OUTDOOR EFFECTS,
MOTOR CARS, ETC.   778—1006

At RIVINGTON HALL.

SIXTH DAY.—Monday, November 16th.

PICTURES, DRAWINGS AND PRINTS.
1057—1216

SEVENTH DAY.—Tuesday, November 17th.

OLD BLUE AND WHITE NANKIN CHINA,
EARLY ENGLISH FURNITURE, ETC.
1217—1353

SAMPLES OF CATALOGUE ITEMS AND THEIR REALIZATION PRICES
(SEE FOLLOWING ILLUSTRATION OF THE UNDERMENTIONED LOTS)

FLEMISH TAPESTRY - LOT 382	£2,.400
JACOBEAN OAK CHEST - LOT 496	£63.0.0
OLD ENGLISH BRACKET CLOCK - LOT 516	£42..0.0
PAIR CHINESE BRONZE KOROS - LOT 522	£12.12.0
PERSIAN CIRCULAR CARPET - LOT 576	£325.10.0
PAIR ADAM WALL MIRRORS - LOT 585	£52.10.0
PAIR EARLY ITALIAN GATES - LOT 589	£27.06.0
PAIR ADAM WALL MIRRORS - LOT 592	£31.10.0

Tapestry and Carpet in Ballroom.   Lot 382.   Lot 576.

Lot 585.   Lot 589.   Lot 592.

Lot 496.   Lot 516.   Lot 522.

The catalogue for the sale of the Leverhulme collections contains 1,353 lots, including examples of Old English furniture from Chippendale, Heppelwhite and Sheraton, antique needlework pictures, tapestries, paintings by many famous artists including Gainsborough, Sir John Lavery, R.A., Erskine Nichol, R.S.A., modern furniture, bedroom equipment, outside effects, motor vehicles etc. etc.

William Hulme Lever, D.Litt., succeeded his father as the second 'Viscount Leverhulme'. He was born on the 25th March 1888, being 37 years old on the death of his father. A married man with one son and two daughters he was then acting chairman of Lever brothers Limited. It seems that the second Viscount had many things in common with his father except perhaps the same degree of affection towards that lovely, lonely moorland home, 'The Bungalow, Rivington, Lancashire. The son's affection for his father is evinced by two tall polished granite pillars which stand on either side of the entrance to Lever Park, Horwich. They were erected in 1934 to commemorate the gift of Lever Park by his father and are appropriately inscribed.

Entrance to Lever Park Avenue marked by the two polished granite pillars erected in memory of Lord Leverhulme by his son in 1934.

Chapter 11 - John Magee - The Second Owner

The new owner of 'The Bungalow', John Magee, was an entirely different personality than Lord Leverhulme. His family ran the Magee Marshall Brewery Company Limited who operated from the 'Crown Brewery' in Derby Street, Bolton.

The firm was founded by David Magee in 1853 and the original brewery, completed in 1866, was considerably extended during 1875. Daniel Marshall ran a brewery in Brown Street, Bolton which Magee purchased in 1885 and three years later the joint concern was formed into a limited company.

Magee Marshall Limited were taken over in November 1958 by the old established firm of Greenall Whitley Limited of Warrington but the Derby Street Brewery continued production until the 2nd October 1970, when it was closed as part of a plan to increase the efficiency of production and distribution within the group.

Before the 1958 take over by Greenalls 250 licensed premises in and around Bolton, Wigan, Blackpool and Southport were controlled by Magee Marshall Limited. Their beer incidentally was brewed with water from Burton-on-Trent, 14 tank wagons, each carrying 60 - 90 barrels a time, regularly ran between Bolton and Burton-on-Trent where the firm had their own well and only the flowers of hops were used in brewing.

'The Bungalow' was intended for use as a week-end home by the Magee family and also as a sort of recreational and welfare centre for employees who were allowed to take advantage of the facilities for bowling matches etc. It was also decided to continue the practice of opening the grounds to visitors on occasions and allow the ballroom to be used for social functions.

After John Magee bought 'The Bungalow' the gardening staff was reduced to just five in number, one of whom was wholly employed in the kitchen gardens. Little was seen of the new owner at first except for brief visits using a company car for transport. As time went on his stays became longer so he bought himself a brand new Armstrong Siddeley motor car which he had delivered to his 'home' in Rivington. John Magee instructed Bob Whittaker, an employee who lived in Bolton Lodge, to act as his chauffeur and there followed a 'crash' driving course because he had never been behind the wheel of a car in his life before.

In spite of marked disinterest at first the Magee family gradually grew to appreciate the amenities provided by 'The Bungalow' and it eventually became very popular amongst them and also the Co-Directors of the Brewery. A niece of John Magee, Miss Cynthia Weaver, prevailed upon him to have tennis courts laid at 'The Bungalow' so that she could indulge her passion for the game; and managed to persuade her uncle to use the smaller section of the Great Lawn for this purpose. Lord Leverhulme had plans to convert this area of lawn into a second lake to provide a further head of water for the waterfalls but the proposal fell through after his death.

Contractors were employed in making two shale tennis courts, the first priority being the laying of an access road from the main drive. The work was done with pick and shovel, as the age of the 'mechanical digger' had not arrived, and on completion the estate gardeners were left to tidy and re-landscape the area.

The Directors of the Brewery were quick to realise the potential of the bungalow grounds as a ready source of materials to landscape the gardens and bowling greens of their more popular public houses. Once again John Magee was persuaded to agree to this suggestion. It seems that he was a benign, genial and somewhat absent minded man whose generosity it was easy to take advantage of.

One decision that John Magee made which he had cause to regret was to allow the local Hunt to hold their annual ball in 'The Bungalow' ballroom. The event degenerated into a drunken revel and so much damage was caused that the staff took weeks to clear up the resultant mess. The employees were so incensed that after pressure from them he withdrew further patronage to this body.

The grounds were the scene of many garden parties the largest event being the World Jamboree of the Scout Movement. Apparently it took the estate gardeners a few years to restore the turf on the great lawn to its original state after hundreds of tents had been pitched there for a week or so.

On the 13th July 1928 a Royal Air Force Bristol Bulldog Fighter crashed into Winter Hill in dense mist. The solitary occupant of this twin-seater plane, Flying Officer Walker, having survived the impact, managed to make his way to Belmont Lodge, despite a broken arm and leg, to raise the alarm. When news broke the grounds were once again in the limelight and received much publicity.

John Magee was not a young man when he bought 'The Bungalow' and during his period of ownership there were no major alterations or additions made to the property. Following John's death, Thomas Magee was appointed executor of his estate and put 'The Bungalow' up for sale.

Chapter 12 - Demolition

There was a widespread feeling that the property should be secured for the benefit of the people of the surrounding district. The idea was first mooted to Horwich Council by the clerk, Mr. Jas Seddon, and in January 1938 a meeting was held of representative local authorities - Horwich, Blackrod, Bolton, Adlington and Chorley Rural District Council. Representatives of Wigan and Aspull attended later meetings and on February 9th 1939, a letter was read from Mr. P. A. Barnes, Secretary of the Council for the Preservation of Rural England who pledged support in the matter. Thomas Magee wrote to the Joint Committee expressing pleasure at their proposal to buy 'The Bungalow' and, in spite of two other prospective buyers, the Committee were offered first option to purchase for the price of £7,000.

The property was freehold but Liverpool Corporation had imposed a condition that 'The Bungalow' should not be used for any purpose than that of a dwelling house. This restriction effactually stultified ideas for its development as a hotel or convalescent home which had been discussed.

With typical dilatoriness the Joint Committee appointed a sub-committee with three objectives; first, to see if Thomas Magee would accept a lower offer, secondly, to interview representatives of Liverpool Corporation regarding the imposed limitations on use of 'The Bungalow' and, thirdly, to prepare an estimate, as far as possible, of the cost of maintaining the property.

Before any replies were received, Bolton Parks Committee informed Horwich Council that they were withdrawing from the negotiations and the decision was ratified by Bolton Town Council at a meeting held on 5th April 1939.

Despite requests to reconsider their decision on the grounds that this valuable amenity would be of most benefit to the people of Bolton, and the cost of upkeep only amounted to $\frac{1}{2}$d in the £ on the rates, Bolton Corporation chose not to reply.

Liverpool Corporation would not alter the conditions on use of 'The Bungalow' saying that it was a long established policy, firmly adhered to previously, of limiting the use of land in the neighbourhood of waterworks. It was regretted that no exception could be made in this case.

The outbreak of World War II meant that Local Authorities could not obtain a loan from the Ministry except for essential purposes, and buying 'The Bungalow' did not fall into this special category. A final appeal was made to Thomas Magee to defer the sale until such time as the Councils were in a position to purchase the property but this was not possible, and so Liverpool Corporation succeeded in acquiring the property for the measly sum of £3,000.

The Dovecote is minus its thatch and all the windows have been boarded up to prevent theft and damage.

It is difficult to imagine that this was once the beautifully furnished Morning Room.

The fixtures and fittings were of such superior quality that many were further utilised elsewhere after The Bungalow was demolished.

The spiral staircase on the left led from the Winter Garden onto the flat roof of 'The Bungalow'. Picture taken during demolition (1948).

During the war years 'The Bungalow' was used as a billet for troops. There was a dormitory in the ballroom and the movement of beds etc. resulted in many of the parquetry blocks being ripped up during this occupation and much wanton damage was caused generally.

The Barns incidentally were used for the storage of sugar and a series of 'nissen-huts' were erected on either side of the driveway leading to Rivington Hall, which was also used for storage purposes. (Harold Dickinson of Horwich was responsible for removing these huts after the war).

Accepting that much damage was caused to 'The Bungalow' during occupation by the armed forces, it must also be remembered that John Magee had tenanted the place just prior to the outbreak of war. Therefore, it could reasonably be argued that, because the house was habitable before the army moved in, then the condition of the dwelling when the troops left was their responsibility and compensation was claimable for any damage from the Government. Whether any amount was paid, or indeed ever claimed, is not known but one thing is certain, there was no money ever spent on repair work at 'The Bungalow'.

In May 1947, Liverpool Corporation announced its plans to demolish 'The Bungalow' stating that the building was a menace to the water supply in its present state and that renovation costs would be upwards of £20,000.

Following an initial reaction of shocked indignation, a number of stated 'resolute' intentions came to nothing - the road to Hell is paved with good intentions - so the demolition contractor was ordered to move in.

'The Bungalow' had been built to last and to lay the walls low was no easy task. The ballroom ceiling resisted even the explosives and there was finally no alternative but to sledge hammer it down.

Following demolition, the grounds were plundered of many exotic shrubs and trees, sections of the lawn were rolled up and taken away and Mother Nature began her own reclamation work.

Dining Room - The broken window and damaged flooring give an idea of the extent of neglect.

*The broken trellis work lying on the lawn border is from the Winter Garden running along
the north front of 'The Bungalow'. (Circa 1947)*

Demolition of South Lodge.

The Crown Hotel, Horwich - a Magee Marshall house. This was the terminus for trams carrying visitors to Lever Park.

Chapter 13 - The Bungalow Grounds - Present Day

The bungalow grounds are currently owned by the North West Water Authority, which corporate body was formed in April 1974, following Local Government re-organisations. Since taking over from Liverpool Corporation, there has been renewed interest in the once proud beauty of the place. In 1975, the Water Authority offered a grant of £2,500 when asking the British Trust for Conservation Volunteers to clear the choked pathways, which had become almost impenetrable, and generally tidy the gardens for public use. It was soon realised that the initial grant fell far short of the expenditure required and a further £7,000 was committed to cover work over a period terminating in March 1977.

Progress in reclamation and clearing the grounds has been subject to the vicissitudes of the economic climate. High unemployment and constraints on Local Government spending have proved an advantage in that the ranks of volunteers have been swelled by those out of work wanting to use their time beneficially; whilst schemes sponsored by Central Government such as 'work experience' and 'youth opportunity' have led to supervised youngsters carrying out clearance projects.

It is extremely difficult to appreciate the dimensions of 'The Bungalow' because all that remains is an area of black and white tiles which were the flooring to lavatories situated near the entrance to the ballroom on the east side of the property. By following the arc created by the edge of the tiles it is possible to make out the circle which once contained the ballroom floor.

Whilst a number of the garden features remain virtually untouched, there is no clue left to indicate the existence of others. Lever's Bridge and many of the paved walkways were ignored during demolition and have subsequently weathered well, but I was surprised to learn that a second pigeon tower, square in design with a four gabled roof, once stood at the end of the pergola extending in front of 'The Bungalow'. The length of the pergola proved another intriguing discovery.

The summerhouses are in a dilapidated state and extremely dirty internally after years of neglect, although it is still possible to stand on the observation plateaux. The loggia (open sided gallery or arcade) below the pigeon tower are in a dangerous condition and notices are presently displayed warning people that they are unsafe. The Pigeon Tower has been fully renovated.

Weeds and shrubs have overgrown much of the great lawn but the square lawn, just below the bungalow site, is still relatively flat. The orchestra steps remain and the stone base, which once supported the sun dial, is diagonally opposite.

Waterfalls, rocky pools and small lakes blend into the natural surroundings and the large 'Japanese' lake is an ever popular venue for visitors. It seems that there are no fish in this lake possibly because the acidity of the water is affected by the peat on the moors.

Schemes have been discussed to open up the area by improving the access roads which are currently so uneven that it is impossible to travel along them in a car; although they are negotiable by the 'Land Rover' type of vehicle. This idea would have an adverse effect in that it could well attract the commercial speculator and the wild isolated appeal of the place would be lost. Fortunately, this notion appears to have been 'shelved', for the time being at least, because a locked metal barrier, placed across the entrance from Sheep House Lane, prevents unauthorised vehicular access. A similar barrier has been put across the entrance to the grounds where Belmont Lodge once stood.

Public conveniences have been erected near the site of Belmont Lodge, which were a much needed amenity. It is a pity that because of the activities of mindless vandals, the toilets must be locked at certain times when unattended to prevent them being rendered unusable.

Attention has been focused on the grounds in general and a great deal of improvement work has been carried out. Pathways have been cleared by cutting back the rhododendrons, fencing and walling has been repaired and sections of handrail constructed along the more precipitous stairways. The most untidy aspect of the gardens are the prolific rhododendron shrubs which, although beautiful in spring and early summer when adorned with multi-coloured blooms, provide an impenetrable barrier to many sections with their tangled branches. There is still a veritable jungle to work at and those pessimists who laughed at the idea of anything other than the native heather and bilberry growing there "should see them now".

Upkeep of the grounds is a costly ongoing commitment and great credit is due to the landowners and the various agencies responsible for financing and carrying out conservation work which is done for very little reward or appreciation in many cases. Without their activities we would lose much of our local heritage.

The recurring sentiment amongst those people to whom I have spoken was - "It is a shame that they ever pulled it down - it was a lovely place". 'The Bungalow' has gone forever but the grounds still provide the fascinating exercise of re-creating in the 'mind's eye' what shape and form these beautiful gardens once took.

Chapter Fourteen - Conclusion

It has been my purpose in the foregoing chapters to give a realistic impression of how 'Roynton Cottage' and 'The Bungalow' once looked. To describe and position the garden features in the grounds, and include reference to Lever Park, have been secondary issues. Inevitably, there are gaps in the story which it has proved impossible to fill because information was unavailable, but I feel sure that there is sufficient material included to facilitate the reader a reasonable level of understanding.

The story is an interesting one coloured with its share of incidents and the central characters include not one but two 'villains'. Edith Rigby who burned down 'Roynton Cottage' was the first, a courageous, if misguided, lady for whom it is difficult not to harbour a sneaking admiration. The second is Liverpool Corporation who took the decision to demolish 'The Bungalow' and robbed future generations of enjoying the 'gem' of the creation. It could also be argued that the Local Councils were 'guilty by default' in not pursuing more vigorously the purchase of this property for the price of £7,000, which would only serve as a deposit on a small terraced property these days.

It is of little consequence who was ultimately responsible for having 'The Bungalow' demolished and there is no point in an exercise to apportion blame because the fact is that the dwelling no longer exists and it is inconceivable that anyone would ever consider building a similar property there at any time in the future.

We are left with the grounds, which are still beautiful even in an overgrown state, and it cannot be denied that the lakes and waterfalls add enchantment to the place. The whole of this garden was a unique adventure in landscape design. The solution of those problems which it posed during construction will always evoke feelings of admiration for the architects and builders who were responsible for such a successful creation.

Mr. Hitchen, whose firm carried out the demolition work, removed a number of structures to a farm in Ellel, Galgate, near Lancaster. With permission from the present owner, these artifacts may still be seen. The dovecote from in front of 'The Bungalow' currently stands in the garden and although without its thatched covering is inhabited by doves. Garden shelters with their original wood lath seats have been rebuilt in the garden and the wrought iron screen from the musicians gallery is there although in a rusty state. Pergola columns plus some of the original beams and trellis work are there whilst a number of the doors from 'The Bungalow' have been incorporated into a house and barn a short distance from the farm.

With hindsight, the time to purchase 'The Bungalow' was in 1939 from Thomas Magee and this plan failed principally because Bolton Corporation withdrew.

Whilst the last tenant of 'The Bungalow', John Magee, perpetuated the popularity of the residence by opening the grounds to the public and so on, the charm, legend and the special place it holds in people's affection must be attributed to Lord Leverhulme. He has been variously described as a 'Captain of Industry' and a 'Genius' and whilst there is no argument with the former title the latter requires some comment.

Samuel Johnson (1709 - 1784) wrote that "The true genius is a mind of large general powers, accidentally determined to some particular direction". Cutting up the long bars of soap in his father's wholesale grocery business 'accidentally' led Lord Leverhulme to become the leading soap manufacturer of his time and there is ample evidence of his outstanding mental capabilities.

Aristotle (B.C. 384 - 322) said that "great geniuses are melancholy". Following the loss of his wife, Lord Leverhulme was a melancholy man internally and this loneliness was compounded by his almost total deafness.

Echoing Lord Leverhulme's words on the death of his wife - 'without her influence there would have been neither a Port Sunlight, nor a Lever Brothers as we know it today', adds weight to the saying that behind every great man there is an equally great woman.

I shall always enjoy walking in the grounds and I know that this pleasurable pastime is enjoyed by many other people, particularly those who live locally and can visit there regularly. Each Good Friday, Rivington will continue to host the thousands of visitors on their way to the Pike, many of whom will stay in the bungalow grounds and wander to their heart's content through this 'enigmatic' garden; whilst others press on to climb to the top of the Pike. The views from this vantage point are stunning but after savouring the conquering feeling for a short spell one realises that it is much colder there and the desire is to return back down the slopes for home.

Examining Lord Leverhulme's decision to build his home on a mountain, I would be surprised if one man in a million would even contemplate such a project, let alone carry out the idea with such successful results. Rivington has been fortunate that a son of Bolton bore such an allegiance to the countryside where he rambled freely as a boy.

The mists of time will close over this chapter in our local history and the dull memory of 'The Bungalow' and grounds. If anyone in the future should ask about the origins and history of the mountain home of the soap millionaire it would please me that this work went some way towards providing an answer.

A photograph of my wife Andrea, as a child, near to the Upper Rivington Reservoir, which embodies the charm of Rivington 1946.

Bibliography

The following are major works to which I have referred:-

Lord Leverhulme	- The Second Viscount Leverhulme
Lord Leverhulme	- W. P. Jolly
About Rivington	- John Rawlinson
Heather in my Hat	- George Birtill
Anyon Kay's Horwich	- Brian Smith
Rivington	- Phoebe Hesketh
My Aunt Edith	- Phoebe Hesketh
A Short History of the Township of Rivington	- William Ferguson Irvine
The Life and Works of an English Landscape Artist	- Thomas H. Mawson
The Art and Craft of Garden making	- Thomas H. Mawson
Self Help	- Samuel Smiles
Baines History of Lancashire (Salford Hundred)	
The Building of the Beacon Tower on Rivington Pike	- Major G. N. Shawcross

The Bungalow Grounds

(Colour Section)

When the book 'Leverhulme's Rivington' was originally published in March 1984, it was felt that a section containing coloured illustrations would be helpful to the reader in making comparisons between the views showing the gardens when they were carefully tended and maintained, and their appearance following years of neglect. This was not a practical proposition at the time for a variety of reasons but circumstances are now different and it is pleasing to be able to rectify this earlier omission.

Liverpool Corporation Waterworks Authority made the decision to demolish the Bungalow in May 1947. By this time the property had been extensively vandalised and the gardens had been plundered of much exotic plant life. A report appeared in the Bolton Evening News dated Monday, 9th June 1947, containing a letter from S. E. Coupe of Great House, Rivington. The content of this correspondence is interesting in that it gives a contemporary view of the despoilation of the Bungalow grounds. It reads as follows :-

WANTON DESTRUCTION AT RIVINGTON
Gardens Despoiled and Bungalow Damaged

According to an "Evening News" reader who lives at Rivington, vandalism is demolishing the Rivington Bungalow more ruthlessly and with much less dignity than the Liverpool Corporation proposes to do. In a letter to the paper he says the public of Bolton and district has no respect for anything at Rivington, and that the Liverpool Corporation has had a constant uphill fight against this wilful destruction.

The writer of the letter, S. E. Coupe, of Great House, Rivington, has lived in that vicinity for 40 years and has spent many happy hours at the Bungalow during that time. "It will be a great grief to me to see the Bungalow go," he explains, "but still I would rather see it pulled down respectfully than the way it is being pulled down at present."

"Don't blame the Liverpool Corporation for pulling it down," he writes. "Blame the public. The Corporation is only finishing it off and not as quickly or as ruthlessly as the public has done. The Corporation has had an uphill fight all the time. For instance, had they not put big iron gates up at the Liverpool Castle there would have been no castle left because of wanton damage.

"At the Bungalow someone even managed to climb on to the top of the ballroom and crash a large paving stone through the glass dome.

"Paving stones were also pushed into the washbowls, smashing every one as well as every window. Doors have been pulled off their hinges. The floor of the lovely ballroom has been ripped up.

"The gardens they have not been able to pull to pieces quickly enough. During this fine weather it has grieved us to see people carrying branches of the flowering shrubs away from the grounds. Recently, I saw a party from Bolton, each of them loaded with rhododendrons, etc. As their ages were between 21 and 50 one could not say they knew no better.

"Someone even thrust a large tree trunk into the overflow pipe of the waterfall. Consequently the water gushed down the hillside and flooded the cottages, my own house included, and Liverpool Corporation had to send a team of men on a Sunday morning to help to bale out—inconvenience for us and expense for Liverpool. The lavatories at the Small Barn are open for the public's convenience, but the majority of people think they are there for destruction purposes. Most of the windows have been smashed and bricks have been thrown into the cisterns.

"Liverpool seem loath to prosecute and if they did they would be called mean and highhanded. Yet it's hard that they should have to spend their own rate-payers' money for the convenience of people around here and that's the thanks they get.

"Recently while the caretaker at Rivington Hall was away a short time on his round of inspection someone broke into the grounds and, I understand, broke about 30 small panes in one large window."

In a talk with an "Evening News" representative an official of the Liverpool Waterworks Department confirmed that the department has had much trouble from hooliganism in the Rivington district. . . . .

Looking across the Upper Rivington Reservoir from the Street, three landmarks can be seen on the horizon, namely (left to right) The Winter Hill Transmitter Mast, The Pigeon Tower and Rivington Pike Tower. The dense growth stretching to the right from the Pigeon Tower hides the Bungalow grounds. (1998)

Towards A New Millenium

Since the Bungalow was demolished, the garden areas have been largely abandoned and rhododendron shrubs have proliferated making many areas inaccessible. At various times, conservation work has been carried out by volunteers resulting in increased access to the grounds. In addition, a number of the garden structures have been maintained and damaged stonework has been restored.

The North West Water Authority commissioned a study to assess the feasibility of a partial restoration of the Bungalow grounds and the reconstruction of a number of garden features, including the tea-houses once sited by the lake in the Japanese Gardens. The project also assessed the situation concerning Lever Park. Work commenced in November 1995 and the terms of reference supplied to the working party were :- 'To provide outline recommendations for the restoration of the Rivington Terraced Gardens and to co-ordinate the production of a complementary Lever Park Master Plan'. It was considered that the proposed scheme could qualify for Millennium funding. In the event, the recommendations of the working party were not accepted and the matter was thus effectively 'shelved'. All relevant matters were carefully considered by the working party and their proposals were costed. Much effort was spent in 'selling' the scheme to the local populace. However, not everyone agreed with the recommendations put forward the chief reason being that the free and unrestricted access to both Lever Park and Bungalow grounds seemed to be under threat.

There is no doubt that a degree of ongoing maintenance to the Bungalow grounds is essential, if only to ensure the safety of visitors. It seems that, for the time being at least, conservation volunteers will once again be called upon to fill the vacuum.

The section following, contains coloured photographs, copies of works of art and illustrations of Roynton Cottage, the Bungalow and grounds. There are difficulties in taking photographs because the dense growth in the grounds often hides completely areas of the garden and its attendant features. A number of the photographs were taken during the 1970s and 1980s when some conservation work had been done and this is evident in the prints. Several of the colour inclusions were taken this year (1998).

View from the Rivington Bungalow by Sir Alfred East, R.A., R.I., P.R.B.A., R.P.E. (1849-1913).

Leslie Cant of Preston painted this view of the Bungalow and grounds as it may have appeared in the 1930s.

All that remains of the second Bungalow are a number of tiled areas on the actual site. The black and white tiles pictured comprised the flooring of toilets adjacent to the ballroom. The circular ballroom area can be traced by projecting the arc created by the edging tiles.

LODGE HOUSES

Stone House Lodge

Two stone pillars are the only clue to the location of Stone House Lodge. (1982)

Belmont Lodge

Belmont Lodge site can also be identified by the two stone gate pillars marking this entrance to the Bungalow grounds. (1982)

Bolton Lodge

Bolton Lodge stood to the left where public conveniences have since been built. Similar stone pillars to those at Stone House Lodge and Belmont Lodge mark the entrance. (1982)

South Lodge

This is the site of South Lodge, very little of which was left following demolition. (1982)

The 'Orchestra' Lawn

During 1982 when this photograph of the 'orchestra' lawn was taken, it still appeared relatively flat but it is presently covered with dense vegetation. A sun-dial was situated in the top left hand corner of the lawn.

'Orchestra' steps

A long flight of rounded steps led from the Bungalow to the lawn at the north front. On a summer evening, dances were held on the lawn and on these occasions the musicians assembled on the steps to provide accompaniment. The steps thus became known as the 'Orchestra' steps. (1982)

Sun-dial

The Bungalow was sited on the 1,000 foot contour of Rivington Moor near to a favourite picnic spot frequented by Lord Leverhulme during his courtship. The actual spot was marked by a sun-dial which contained a plaque bearing the legend 'Live today, not regretting yesterday nor fearing tomorrow'. All that presently remains is the base of the sun-dial. (1998)

Garden features

A complex system of stone pathways led from the Bungalow site to the 'Orchestra' lawn and the lower gardens. The Pigeon Tower can be seen in the background. (1982)

These two photographs show the general area of terracing leading from the Bungalow site. (1982)

Flights of stone steps and archways throughout the garden areas, have generally survived well over the years despite a total lack of maintenance. (1982)

The Pigeon Tower

A screening wall extends from the Pigeon Tower and this once contained nesting boxes for bird-life.

A view of the Pigeon Tower and screening wall from the terracing. (1976)

The distinctive stone plinth on the right once supported the statue of a boy with dolphins. The Pigeon Tower is visible to the left. (1980)

A disused quarry near to the Pigeon Tower was used in Lord Leverhulme's time as a garage area for the estate vehicles. (1982)

The Kitchen Gardens

The kitchen gardens stretched behind Stone House Lodge and a photograph of them when they were in use has, so far, proved illusive. At the right of this walkway was a bothy and other buildings for use by the gardeners. (1982)

Remains of the kitchen gardens looking towards Stone House Lodge. (1982)

Remains of the stone bothy used by the gardeners. The Pike Tower can be seen in the background. (1982)

Lever's Bridge

The arched bridge in the Bungalow grounds. (1976)

Japanese Lake

A peaceful scene looking across the Japanese Lake. (1982)

This distinctive bridge spans the waterfall above the Japanese Lake. There were once handrails on either side of the bridge. (1982)

The Great Lawn

In order to show the amount of stone which had to be quarried for the great lawn a section of the underlying bedrock was left at its original level and protrudes about 7 feet above the lawn surface. The rock can be seen top centre. At the present time brambles and bilberry bushes almost cover the rock. (1982)

Summerhouses

Summer house on the great lawn. This structure is difficult to distinguish from the summer house in the smaller section of the lawn. The main difference is that the window on the right retains a stone mullion. The greenery in front of this summer house has grown so much over the years that it is presently impossible to obtain a similar view. (1982)

A distance view of the summer house on the smaller section of the great lawn converted into a tennis court by John Magee. (1982)

In this close-up view of the same summer house the damage to the stonework can be seen but the structure remains basically sound. (1982)

Situated just below the Pigeon Tower, this summer house remains in a reasonable condition. (1976)

The three arches are all that remain of one of the summerhouses situated on the terracing just below the Pigeon Tower. (1976)

Waterfalls in the Lower Dell

Taken in December 1982, this photograph of a waterfall in the Lower Dell is presently difficult to obtain because of dense vegetation.

View of the waterfall from above. (1982)

Garden Ornaments

Following the demolition of the Bungalow a number of stone structures were removed by the contractor for safe keeping. It was purely by chance that a number of these artefacts were subsequently located and permission was afforded for them to be photographed.

One of the most significant structures to be preserved at Ellel is the dove cote which once stood in front of the Bungalow. Despite lacking its thatched roof the structure is easily identifiable and was still used for its original purpose. (1982)

The author inspecting pergola columns from the Bungalow during 1982 at Ellel, Galgate.

143

Lever Park Avenue from Scholes Bank, Horwich. The two granite pillars, erected in memory of Viscount Leverhulme by his son, stand at either side of the entrance to Lever Park. the pillars are inscribed as follows :- (Left hand pillar) - 'LEVER PARK - THE GIFT OF WILLIAM HESKETH LEVER - 1st VISCOUNT LEVERHULME - BORN AT 6 WOOD STREET, BOLTON, SEPTEMBER 19TH 1851. DIED AT HAMPSTEAD, LONDON. MAY 7TH 1925. - FOR THE BENEFIT OF THE CITIZENS OF HIS NATIVE TOWN AND NEIGHBOURHOOD BY ACT OF PARLIAMENT IN 1902 THE OWNERSHIP AND CARE OF THE PARK WERE VESTED IN THE CORPORATION OF THE CITY OF LIVERPOOL.'
(Right hand pillar) - 'LEVER PARK - THESE PYLONS WERE ERECTED BY WILLIAM HULME 2nd VISCOUNT LEVERHULME TO COMMEMORATE THE GIFT OF LEVER PARK BY HIS FATHER 1934'.

The author at Ellel, Galgate with one of the oak doors from the Bungalow. (1982)

A concrete lantern from the Japanese Lake at the Rivington Bungalow.

APPENDICES

Mr Ernest Shone, who was the Estate Factor for Lord Leverhulme, received many written instructions from his employer. Fortunately, Mr Shone's family have preserved a number of these letters and they are reproduced below by kind permission of his daughter-in-law, Mrs Mary Shone, and her two sons Christopher and Stephen. The content of the letters is self-explanatory.

Ernest Shone – Lord Leverhulme's Estate Factor

THE HILL,
HAMPSTEAD HEATH.
NORTH END.
LONDON, N.W.3.

27th November 1922.

Mr. E. Shone,
Stone Lodge,
Rivington,
Nr. Bolton. Lancs.

Dear Mr. Shone,

I have a note from Mr. Hermon Crook the Architect who is acting for the Ball Room I am putting on the site of the present Garth. He writes me that they are now ready to commence, and that the plants etc., in the Garth should be removed. Please see to this at once.

Any further instructions in connection with work that Mr. Hermon Crook may require, it will be quite right for you to act upon without referring to myself.

Yours sincerely,

Leverhulme

TELEPHONE CITY 5740
TELEGRAMS "LEVERBRO
FLEET LONDON"

Lever House   JH/ML/B.
Blackfriars
LONDON E.C. 4

20th June 1923.

Mr. E. Shone,
Stone House,
The Bungalow,
Rivington,
Nr. Bolton, Lancs.

Dear Mr. Shone,

In reply to your letter of the 16th instant, I am quite willing for Ice-cream carts to stand on the road between the Grammar School and "The Bungalow" on the day when the Horwich Combined Charities hold their Fete, but I cannot of course allow them to be in the grounds.

Yours sincerely,

Leverhulme

DICTATED BY LORD LEVERHULME

LEWS CASTLE.
STORNOWAY.

Telegrams,
LEVERHULME, STORNOWAY.

24th August, 1923.

Mr. Shone,
The Bungalow,
Rivington,
Near Bolton,
Lancs.

Dear Mr. Shone,

With reference to the three representatives of the ancient British cattle which I have now sent to Lever Park, the enclosed information which my Secretary, Mr. Evans, has dug out for me on a visit to the British Museum, will be of interest.

Yours sincerely,

Leverhulme

COMPAGNIE BELGE MARITIME DU CONGO

SOCIÉTÉ ANONYME

Siège Social:
ANVERS

Adr. Télégr.:
"BELCONGO" ANVERS

VAPEUR "_____"

LE _____ 19__

Dear McMahon

We are having
a magnificent voyage
not been unwell
in over 2 days —
Kindest regards
Dyou & Peter &

Dear Lawrence &

Mrs Fred Heather
had sent &
posted to
Dr Foshan
Rome Silver
Boothbay Harbor
Maine
United States
Please have
some sent + post
already done to
con McMahon
several your

Dear Lawrence
Dyou Fred Heas
lovely colume
has Mule Heather
Seeds have come
up as healthier
Please let her
have a cheery
or two of white
heather
Hoping you are
all well
Yours sincerely
Catherine

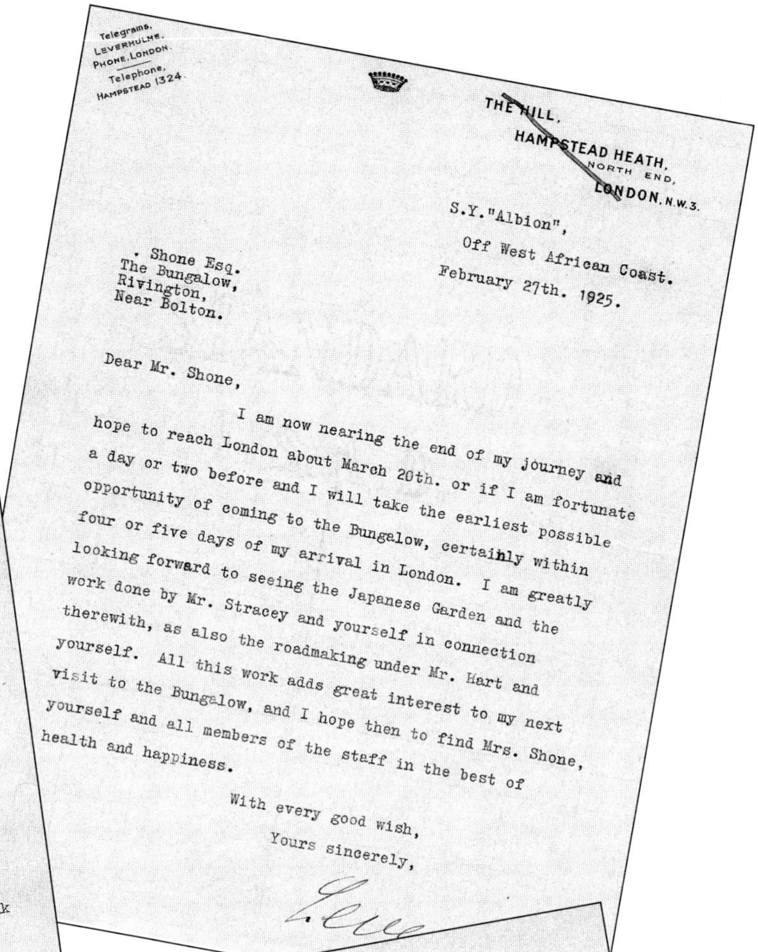

Letter 1 (top right):

Telegrams,
LEVERHULME,
PHONE. LONDON.
Telephone,
HAMPSTEAD 1324.

THE HILL,
HAMPSTEAD HEATH,
NORTH END.
LONDON. N.W.3.

S.Y. "Albion",
Off West African Coast.
February 27th. 1925.

. Shone Esq.
The Bungalow,
Rivington,
Near Bolton.

Dear Mr. Shone,

I am now nearing the end of my journey and hope to reach London about March 20th. or if I am fortunate a day or two before and I will take the earliest possible opportunity of coming to the Bungalow, certainly within four or five days of my arrival in London. I am greatly looking forward to seeing the Japanese Garden and the work done by Mr. Stracey and yourself in connection therewith, as also the roadmaking under Mr. Hart and yourself. All this work adds great interest to my next visit to the Bungalow, and I hope then to find Mrs. Shone, yourself and all members of the staff in the best of health and happiness.

With every good wish,
Yours sincerely,

Letter 2 (left):

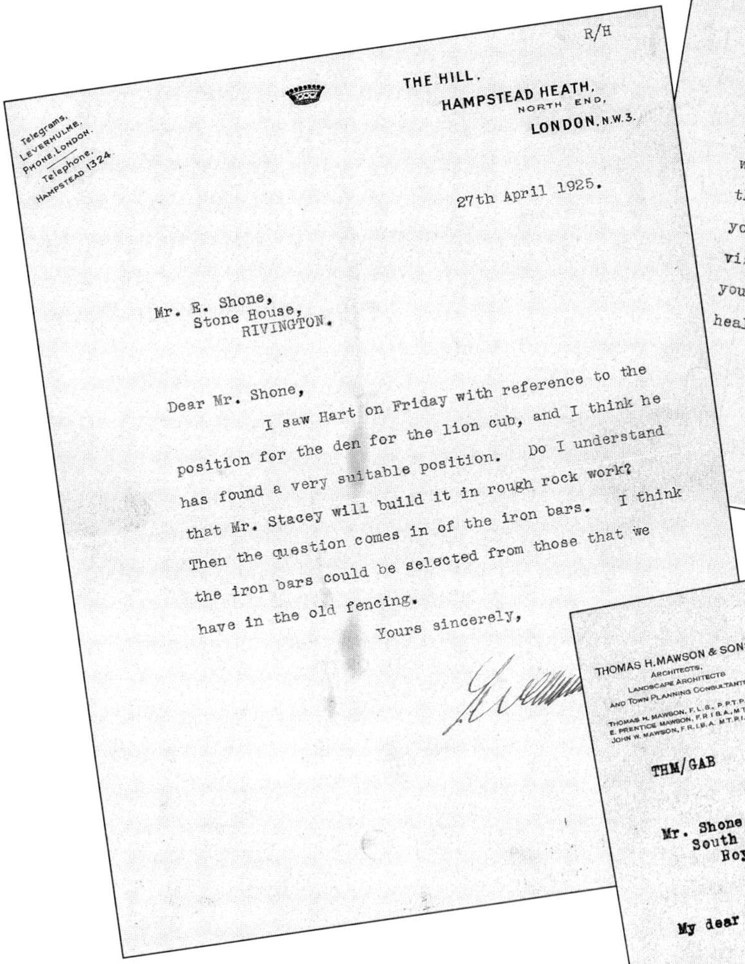

R/H

THE HILL,
HAMPSTEAD HEATH,
NORTH END,
LONDON. N.W.3.

Telegrams,
LEVERHULME,
PHONE. LONDON.
Telephone,
HAMPSTEAD 1324.

27th April 1925.

Mr. E. Shone,
Stone House,
RIVINGTON.

Dear Mr. Shone,

I saw Hart on Friday with reference to the position for the den for the lion cub, and I think he has found a very suitable position. Do I understand that Mr. Stacey will build it in rough rock work? Then the question comes in of the iron bars. I think the iron bars could be selected from those that we have in the old fencing.

Yours sincerely,

Letter 3 (bottom right):

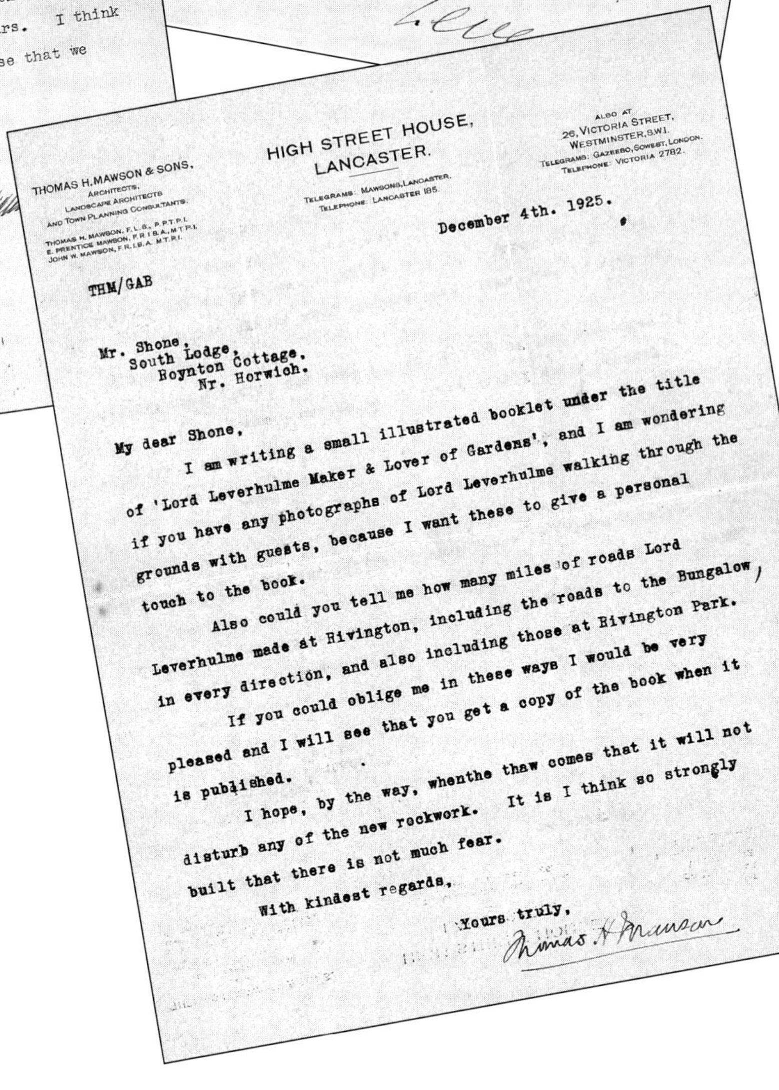

THOMAS H. MAWSON & SONS,
ARCHITECTS.
LANDSCAPE ARCHITECTS
AND TOWN PLANNING CONSULTANTS.

THOMAS H. MAWSON, F.L.S., P.F.T.P.I.
E. PRENTICE MAWSON, F.R.I.B.A. M.T.P.I.
JOHN W. MAWSON, F.R.I.B.A. M.T.P.I.

HIGH STREET HOUSE,
LANCASTER.

TELEGRAMS. MAWSONS, LANCASTER.
TELEPHONE. LANCASTER 195.

ALSO AT
26, VICTORIA STREET,
WESTMINSTER, S.W.I.
TELEGRAMS. GAZEEBO, SOWEST, LONDON.
TELEPHONE VICTORIA 2782.

December 4th. 1925.

THM/GAB

Mr. Shone,
South Lodge,
Hoynton Cottage,
Nr. Horwich.

My dear Shone,

I am writing a small illustrated booklet under the title of 'Lord Leverhulme Maker & Lover of Gardens', and I am wondering if you have any photographs of Lord Leverhulme walking through the grounds with guests, because I want these to give a personal touch to the book.

Also could you tell me how many miles of roads Lord Leverhulme made at Rivington, including the roads to the Bungalow, in every direction, and also including those at Rivington Park.

If you could oblige me in these ways I would be very pleased and I will see that you get a copy of the book when it is published.

I hope, by the way, whenthe thaw comes that it will not disturb any of the new rockwork. It is I think so strongly built that there is not much fear.

With kindest regards,

Yours truly,
Thomas H Mawson

ISLAND OF LEWIS.

OFFERED TO THE PEOPLE BY LORD LEVERHULME.

WITH CASTLE, PARK; AND SHOOTING LODGES.

A joint meeting of public bodies convened at the request of Viscount Leverhulme was held at Stornoway yesterday, when his lordship announced that he is quitting Lewis and made an amazing offer of the whole island to the people as a free gift.

In the course of a lengthy statement, telegraphs our correspondent, Lord Leverhulme said he never had a more uncongenial burden laid upon him than the one that devolved upon him that day, which was to explain fully and without reserve the position he found himself placed in with regard to his relationship with the Island of Lewis. As he explained when he first came to the island he had not been attracted to it by any love of sport, but entirely by the possibilities he thought he recognized in Lewis of doing something for the permanent benefit of the people of the island. Speaking of his large schemes for the development of the fisheries which involved an immense amount of money, the improvement of Stornoway harbour alone being estimated at half a million, he emphasized the point that this work was not being made at Governement expense nor were the Government ever asked to make any grant or subsidy towards the costs

STUBBORN BOARD OF AGRICULTURE.

If the schemes were a success there might be a possibility of his being recouped for the expenditure, but if they were a failure the whole burden would fall upon himself. Therefore he made it an absolute condition that unless he could have ten years' free and uninterrupted time for the success of his experiments he must decline to commence. He had hoped that the advantages of his schemes, both in the expenditure of large sums of money during constructions and the possibility of further employment after construction, would have been so obvious that the Board of Agriculture would have changed their policy for the breaking of the farms into small holdings until at least he had had a ten years' trial period for his schemes. The Board of Agriculture, however, did not change, and so all his industrial schemes had to be finally abandoned, but he still clung to his town-planning scheme for Stornoway, because he felt the people of Stornoway should not suffer merely because he could not proceed with the development of the island as a fishing centre. He had now arrived at the final phase which prevented him proceeding even with that work which would have been of outstanding pleasure and interest to himself and, he had hoped, not without equal pleasure and still greater profit to the town of Stornoway.

STOPPED TOWN PLANNING SCHEME.

Proceeding, his lordship went into the correspondence that had taken place over an observation made at the Scottish Office to his representative, Sir Edgar Sanders, that it might be necessary to take all the remaining farms in Lewis, except the Manor Farm, unless the demand for crofts was soon satisfied. On realizing the position that must follow upon this prospective action of the Scottish Office, he definitely decided to stop his town planning schemes also. He telegraphed the chamberlain to cease negotiations for the acquisition of further properties under the town planning scheme, and those properties that had been acquired he was willing to resell to the former owners at ten per cent. less than he had paid them for them. This offer would remain open till December 31st.

And now he came to the final summary of his position as he had mentioned in his opening words. He was never attracted to Lewis as a sportsman, and was really, therefore, now left without any object or motive for remaining there. Under these conditions he now proposed to take one of two courses: One would be that he should sell the Castle and all the sporting properties, the other, which would be more congenial to himself would be to make a gift of the whole Island of Lewis as he purchased it from Colonel Mathieson, exclusive of most of the industries he had commenced in Stornoway, and any of the property he had bought since he became proprietor.

THE FARMS AND CROFTS.

He suggested that Lewis should be divided into two spheres of influence, one, including all the lands, etc., lying beyond a radius of seven miles from Stornoway post office, the other being within that area. In the sphere beyond the seven mile radius all existing crofts, including the crofts proposed to be cut out of Galson Farm, but excepting crofts occupied by ex-raiders, would be given as a free gift from himself to their respective cultivators. All farms not yet taken for crofts together with all sporting and fishing rights, with their lodges and houses, together with all crofts in the possession of non-resident crofters, he wished to give to trustees to be nominated jointly by the Lewis District Committee and the voters within the area. With reference to farms and crofts within the seven mile radius, including all portions of the manor farm outside the castle grounds and policies together with all the fishing and sporting rights within these limits, he wished to give to trustees to be nominated by Stornoway Town Council and the voters in the area. To these trustees he wished to give, in addition, Lews Castle and gardens with conservatories, etc., and including the castle policies.

ENDOWED MUNICIPAL BUILDING AND LIBRARY.

The castle itself was to be used as a municipal building and library, and the remainder as a public park and recreation ground, which he would be grateful if the trustees would name the Lady Lever Park, after his late wife, who was with him on his first visit to Stornoway in 1884. There would naturally be certain expenses for the upkeep of the castle and public park greater than was usual for towns of the size of Stornoway, and towards meeting these expenses he proposed to transfer to the trustees the gas works, the fish offal factory, and steam laundry, the profits from which he hoped would prevent any undue burden of costs of upkeep of the castle and policies falling on the rates. He did not include in that gift any of the furnishings, tapestries, etc., of the castle, which would be entirely unsuited for the uses and purposes of a municipal building, but in the gift of the lodges he did include the furniture and fittings. The transfer of the properties, he suggested, should take place as from November if his offer was accepted, and be adjusted as to income and expenditure at that date, so that the trustees and crofters should receive their gifts free of all indebtedness.

HOPES FOR EARLY DECISION.

As he was leaving for Australia in November he would like an early decision as to the acceptance or rejection, and he would like to have a reply not later than October 6th. His earnest wish was that the intended recipients might see their way to accept his offer. The change of ownership should create an entirely different atmosphere and viewpoint which he hoped would all be favourable to the future progress and welfare of the island. Concluding, he said he was leaving it with deep regrets, but carrying with him the happiest recollections of his five years' residence amongst the people of the island, and his most profound gratitude for the full and generous welcome and support he had always received practically unanimously from all, because support and welcome came from all but less than two per cent. of those living in Lewis. He supposed they would receive his proposals as indicating his desire when leaving Lewis to do all in his power to help the future welfare and prosperity and happiness of its people.

Provost Kenneth Mackenzie, who presided, thanked Lord Leverhulme for his princely offer and after his lordship withdrew, he (the Provost) remarked that even the most sceptical among them must realize that by his magnificent offer Lord Leverhulme had that day heaped coals of fire on the heads of the very small percentage of the population who had opposed his schemes. The bodies concerned will meet this week to consider the matter.

Lord Leverhulme left for the south last night.

149

The Funeral of the late

VISCOUNT LEVERHULME

will take place on

MONDAY, THE 11TH MAY, 1925

AT CHRIST CHURCH, PORT SUNLIGHT

preceded by a SERVICE at 1-45 p.m.

THIS CARD MUST BE PRESENTED AT
THE DOOR OF THE CHURCH.

A

(12806 & 15930) 10/24 Harrow F.275 & 1730

B or C.	Charges to pay	POST OFFICE G R TELEGRAPHS.	No. of Telegram
RECEIVED	s. d.		SENT	Office Stamp.

At 2·25 P. M.

From M

By Au

If the receiver of an Inland Telegram doubts its accuracy he may have it repeated on payment of half the amount originally paid for its transmission, and if it be found that there was any inaccuracy the amount paid for repetition will be refunded. Special conditions are applicable to the repetition of Foreign Telegrams.

THIS FORM MUST ACCOMPANY ANY ENQUIRY RESPECTING THIS TELEGRAM.

At .... M
To ....
By ....

HORWICH 27 MY 25 BOLTON

Prefix	Time handed in	Office of Origin and Service Instructions	Words
	1·57 M.	London City P.	29

Shone Care Leverhulme Horwich La...

Necessity of ceasing all developments
forthwith makes any suggestions for
completion of gorge impossible. Stop.
Will be away from tomorrow until
Saturday week. Leverhulme

Suffragist Outrage at Rivington.

Roynton Cottage Burned to the Ground.
Story of a Mysterious Motor-Car.

The once picturesque timbered bungalow, Roynton Cottage, Horwich, one of the most charming residences belonging to Sir William H. Lever, Bart., is to-day but an ugly mass of charred ruin and debris. The terrible transformation was affected in the space of two short hours early on Tuesday. The whole of the residential part of the buildings has been entirely razed to the ground by an incendiarism which has been as effective as it was savage, and not an identifiable vestige of any article of furniture even remains. Four stone main chimney stacks stand gauntly on the Pike headlands, emphasizing the work of destruction that has been carried out. Such devastation, it seems absolutely safe to say, is the wanton achievement of some person or persons actively concerned with the militant suffragist movement. For in all particulars, from the very nature of the fire itself to the discovery of articles and messages near the scene evidencing sympathy with the "Votes for Women" cause, everything indicates the incendiary suffragist. For instance, there has been found on the estate, and since handed to the police, a small bag, very much like a dispatch case. Attached to this was a label upon which was written,

"Mr. McKenna, London, via Horwich."

There was also inside the case a type-written message which is of doubly regrettable import. This sets forth that the act of destruction is "Lancashire's message to the King from the women, 'Votes for women due.'" Then follows: "Message to the King, Liverpool: Wake up the Government. First give us reason to be loyal, and then try us." Also there was found inside the case a pair of lady's grey suede gloves. One, of these. it is stated, was blood-stained and gashed across the hand part as though it had been worn by someone climbing railings, and in which act they had met with accidents and received hurt to the hand. There is also the possibility that the injury might have been sustained when actually setting fire to the building, or in breaking a window when seeking a way into the bungalow. This bag, or case – it is referred to by the police as a card-board suit case with brass fittings and label – was found tied to a fence with string at a point about 120 yards below the cottage occupied by Mr. Rigg, the head gardener on the estate. Another important circumstance is that on Tuesday morning a policeman on scouring the roads about the Pike on a bicycle, discovered comparatively fresh tracks of a motor-car and also a double-headed spanner which is believed to have been dropped from a car, and which might possibly have been used in affecting entrance to the bungalow. A representative of the Bolton "Evening News" visited the scene of the outrage at an early hour this morning, and as the result of investigations ascertained that a very few minutes after the actual discovery of the fire a motor car was heard to pass along the road near to the residence of Mr. Adamson, the residential engineer of the Liverpool Waterworks, which is on the estate in comparatively close proximity to the Roynton Cottage. The supposition is that this Motor-car carried the person or persons who had committed the outrage. There has been found a copy of "The Suffragette" newspaper, dated April 25th, 1913, saturated with paraffin, and with the words written thereon in lead pencil "Sir W.H. Lever cannot." On top of this was a box of matches and the key referred to, so that everything points to the work of the militant suffragists, though workmen on the estate informed our representative, in reply to his queries, that they had not observed any suspicious strangers lurking about the district during the past few days, neither is there any trace of the origin of the fire. The fact that the residence had been fired was first discovered about half-past one o'clock this morning by the watchman connected with the waterworks, who aroused Mr. Adamson and gave the alarm. Mr. Adamson speedily dressed and rushed up the Pike, there to find the bungalow burning fiercely in three or four places on all sides of the building. It was then very evident, said Mr. Adamson, that the fire had been started at each of these points, and that each had taken hold securely. When Mr. Adamson arrived the whole residential part was evidently doomed, for very soon afterwards it was one huge mass of flames. Mr. Jonathan Simpson, who was architect for the whole series of buildings, told our representative that the residential part was chiefly a timbered structure, and that the flames and the heat must have been intense. Some idea of the terrific nature of the heat may be gathered from a view of the huge iron beams which were constructed in the building. These are twisted and bent into all sorts of grotesque shapes. One huge iron girder which had spanned the residential part had bent almost double. Indeed, the interior of the place whilst the fire was raging must have been very much like

A Huge Furnace.

At such a high altitude – one of the loftiest points in Lancashire, being 1,000 feet above sea level – and in so exposed a position, the flames would be fanned exceedingly by the night breezes, and to this, of course, must be added the fact that the woodwork, chiefly of pine, was highly inflammable. It was little, of course, that Mr. Adamson himself could do to try and check the flames. He raised the employees living in the lodges at various parts of the estate, and also he got into telephonic communication with the Horwich Fire Station. The Horwich L. and Y. Fire Brigade, however, do not attend fires in Rivington, this being outside their recognized boundary.

Neither also did the Chorley brigade respond to a later call for the same reason. Chief Officer Semple, of the Horwich Brigade, however, responded unofficially in person, and on arrival at the cottage – this about 2.30 – he directed the operations of a number of men who had rushed to the place on observing the flames, to the saving of the beautiful garth, or enclosed garden, and the building on the south side of the court. A length of hose was brought into service, and one jet of water was got into play upon the flames. This was entirely insufficient to extinguish the fire, but was made excellent service of to save the garth and outbuildings. These outbuildings are largely constructed of stone. Whilst attention was directed to saving these the whole of the house part was being gutted, and this portion of the building burned fiercely. One small portion of a side wall is all that remains of the walls, outer or partition. A number of men employed at the Loco Works had observed the conflagration and, proceeding to the spot, they rendered valuable assistance in the work of salvage. But they were unable to prevent damage estimated to amount between £15,000 and £20,000, being done before the fire spent itself in the area to which it was confined. With regard to the appeals to the Horwich and Chorley brigades, great praise is due to Ald. James Lawrence, J.P., of Anderton Hall. He observed the fire from his residence, which is situate directly across the park and in full view of Roynton Cottage. He

Hurried to the Cottage

and also telephoned to Horwich and Chorley for the fire brigades. He could not secure connexion with Chorley, however, and therefore he brought out his motor-car and drove over to Chorley, whence he telephoned to Thornton Manor, and thus gave information of the outrage. Sir William and Lady Lever on Monday evening dined with the King and Queen at Knowsley Hall, and only returned to their residence at a late hour. Mr. Lawrence got into communication with Thornton Manor about four o'clock, and about that time the destructive work of the fire had been completed. Mr. Simpson was informed of the fire at about six o'clock, and he promptly visited the scene with Mr. H. Stanley Atherton. They stated that it was fortunate there was no one living in the Cottage at the time, otherwise there would have been no chance of escape, for the flames must have greedily and speedily eaten up the place at all points. As to the household appointments, all that are left behind are bent and twisted fire grates, radiators, and a huge cistern which had crashed down from its supports. The place had been completely razed, walls, and interior,

To Its Very Foundations.

It is next to impossible to trace among the debris how actually the place was ignited, but it would almost appear as if some inflammable liquid had been liberally sprinkled about the rooms before ignition. The scene is one of terrible havoc. Beautiful old furniture, exceedingly valuable tapestry, needlework, and pictures, etc., which had been objects of so much admiration by visitors to the Cottage have been totally destroyed. Of the tapestry nothing remains but pieces of wire netting. The lovely verandah which had overlooked the gardens, is no more. Charred timber is lying about in the shrubbery, and lead has flown all over the place on to the surrounding stonework. The peaceful scene in the garth, where pigeons fluttered unconcernedly about and around the lawn and gardens, was in striking contrast to that on the site of the former cottage adjoining though they be. A stone communicating verandah remains intact, but of the residential part not a portion of the building remains secure. What was the main entrance is indicated merely by a few charred pieces of wood. There is no trace of windows beyond melted lead lights and the ashes of burned wood. At ten o'clock eight and a half hours after the outbreaks, flames repeatedly broke out among the debris, and the jet which had been so serviceable in preventing the spread to the garth, was again serviceable in extinguishing these, a number of workmen associated with the estate being at work under the supervision of Mr. Stanley Atherton. Police also inspected the place, one of the earliest visitors being Inspector Farquharson. The police also searched the grounds for further traces of depredators. As to ingress to the Cottage grounds this is comparatively easy of accomplishment as there are but low railings to surmount. It is supposed that the wearer of the blood-stained glove sustained her injury in climbing the railings. The glove is said to be of rather a large size. A number of people who saw the fire when it was at its height state the sight was a most imposing one, the flames being very vivid, and being observable at a great distance because of the altitude of the conflagration. Cameras were in great request, and many sightseers sought admission to the courtyard of the cottage, but were turned away by the police.

King's Message of Sympathy.

A large number of people visited the Pike on Tuesday, Wednesday, and Thursday in the hope of securing a near view of the fire-destroyed Cottage, but police who were on duty kept the crowds at a distance. A sight of the ruins could, however, be obtained from various places 200 yards and more away, and these view-points were very poplar. Some idea of the great extent of the damage could be conceived even from a distance. The damage, it may be added, is covered by insurance, and representatives of the insurance company visited the scene on Tuesday. The police continue to make exhaustive investigations, but we are informed that there are no developments in this respect, and that the incendiaries have not yet ben traced. Sir William Lever on Tuesday received sympathetic messages regarding his loss from the King and Lord Derby. The message from the King was as follows:–

"Much regret to hear from the newspapers that while you were here (Knowsley) last night your house at Rivington and its contents were destroyed by fire. I sympathize with you in your loss. – George R.I."

Lord Derby telegraphed:–

"Please accept sincere sympathy with you at the loss you have sustained by the burning of your house. A most deplorable thing to have happened."

APPENDIX A.

RIVINGTON RAINFALL.—Years 1849 to 1899.

Station of Gauge	Daily Gauge	Monthly Gauge	Mean of Daily and Monthly Gauges	—	Stones-house No. 1 (Daily)	Game-keeper's (Monthly)	Higher Hill	Game-keeper's New	Great Hill	Hurst Hill	Coppice Stile	Stones-house No. 2	Brown Hill	Lower Knoll	Lower Rivington	Mean of Daily and Monthly Gauges
Latitude. Deg. Min. Sec.	53 38 29	53 48 58¾	—		53 38 29	53	53 41 50½	53 40 58¾	53 39 59	53 39 20½	53 40 1½	53 38 29	53 38 14¾	53 36 41	53 36 30½	
Longitude. Deg. Min. Sec.	2 34 22	2 32 40½	—		2 34 22	2 32 40½	2 31 2¼	2 32 40½	2 32 7¼	2 33 44	2 33 50	2 34 22	2 32 44	2 32 29¼	2 33 26	
Altitude.	750 feet.	725 feet.	—		623 feet.	850 feet.	733 feet.	850 feet.	1240 feet.	1029 feet.	879 feet.	623 feet.	843 feet.	742 feet.	440 feet.	
Year. 1849	—	—	—	Year. 1875	39·67	41·82	33·95	—	—	41·10	37·15	39·65	38·55	—	—	45·41
1850	—	—	—	1876	39·16	45·84	35·45	—	—	41·65	37·40	38·70	39·50	41·35	—	50·83
1851	—	—	—	1877	53·40	64·65	55·70	45·28	—	63·10	53·60	57·30	59·05	57·50	—	47·04
1852	—	—	—	1878	41·18	46·47	40·30	43·25	—	47·60	39·45	42·75	42·45	43·75	—	61·70
1853	37·25	37·25	37·25	1879	38·74	44·32	34·40	44·29	—	44·30	37·35	38·35	39·85	41·15	—	37·25
1854	43·57	43·15	43·36	1880	42·00	45·11	39·75	49·40	—	44·10	40·10	41·05	43·55	42·30	—	43·36
1855	39·35	38·90	39·11	1881	46·65	51·01	40·35	53·61	—	47·30	41·15	45·90	47·05	48·40	—	39·11
1856	50·21	49·00	49·58	1882	49·38	*	45·91	47·62	57·89	51·16	44·90	49·36	49·59	49·76	—	49·58
1857	41·03	41·30	41·14	1883	43·64	—	40·56	39·11	49·62	44·76	39·93	41·68	43·72	44·84	—	41·14
1858	44·75	42·45	43·58	1884	34·48	—	32·69	39·62	39·72	34·42	30·84	33·35	34·12	33·50	—	43·58
1859	47·59	46·10	46·83	1885	39·06	—	34·05	48·14	43·22	38·71	33·22	38·23	37·80	39·36	—	46·83
1860	50·68	51·95	51·29	1886	46·51	—	41·16	39·97	50·68	47·74	41·62	45·35	44·60	45·62	43·34	51·29
1861	45·74	47·02	46·38	1887	28·00	—	26·68	40·56	32·34	29·76	26·23	27·70	26·16	26·98	24·29	46·38
1862	47·94	49·10	48·52	1888	38·83	—	34·05	41·55	44·07	39·75	36·02	37·03	36·02	37·87	34·22	48·52
1863	49·53	52·56	51·04	1889	39·46	—	33·87	48·29	46·28	41·48	37·12	39·03	38·01	38·89	35·65	51·04
1864	39·68	39·81	39·74	1890	43·76	—	39·48	49·67	51·58	47·03	43·20	43·73	43·37	42·15	39·24	39·74
1865	32·51	37·10	34·78	1891	46·45	—	41·38	45·75	54·55	50·43	47·75	45·63	45·21	43·96	40·87	34·78
1866	50·67	57·00	53·83	1892	40·43	—	36·45	41·43	47·13	42·50	42·64	40·53	39·67	41·57	39·32	53·83
1867	40·39	44·50	42·44	1893	37·85	—	35·00	46·81	45·51	42·64	41·85	37·82	37·67	37·08	35·40	42·44
1868	41·60	47·11	44·35	1894	42·72	—	38·13	40·44	50·62	47·45	47·52	42·40	40·92	42·14	40·48	44·35
1869	44·45	49·20	46·82	1895	36·67	—	34·89	45·75	41·85	37·68	37·85	36·45	35·82	35·13	34·26	46·82
1870	41·03	48·55	44·79	1896	43·58	—	37·90	48·56	49·14	43·40	41·98	43·10	42·52	43·43	41·08	44·79
1871	42·70	45·90	44·30	1897	44·08	—	39·02	44·20	47·42	44·32	39·40	43·72	43·96	43·07	40·71	44·30
1872	57·30	61·60	59·45	1898	39·63	—	35·21	43·44	43·63	39·39	35·97	39·30	36·28	38·48	34·71	59·45
1873	38·59	45·65	42·12	1899	41·61	—	35·92	—	41·16	38·15	35·24	41·55	37·00	39·83	38·11	42·12
1874	42·29	50·60	46·44													46·44
Rainfall for 22 years, 1878 to 1899															Mean of 7 Gauges, omitting Great Hill and Lower Rivington. 40·77	Mean of Daily and Monthly Gauges. 42·78

* Old Gauge removed.

The Rivington Works
Watershed and Reservoirs

The Rivington Watershed comprises about 10,000 acres of thinly inhabited hill and moorland on the Millstone Grit Formation, lying between the towns of Bolton and Blackburn, in Lancashire. The elevation ranges from about 450 feet O.D. in the valleys, to 1,500 feet on the hill tops. The principal streams on the watershed are the Roddlesworth, Rake, Yarrow and Douglas, and the rainfall is collected into reservoirs formed by earth embankments carried across the natural valleys. The area and contents of each reservoir and the principal dimensions of the embankments are given in the subjoined table:—

| Name of Reservoir | Area in Acres | Contents in Million Gallons | Embankments | | Width of the Bye Washes. Feet |
			Length Feet	Greatest Depth in Feet	
Roddlesworth, Upper................	26.0	178	1,190	69	69
" Lower	16.4	99.7	590	81	
Rake...	13.8	79.9	1,500	84	98
Anglezarke	191.6	1,019	3,550	46	105
Chorley....................................	10.1	48.3	990	39	20
Rivington	275.0	1,841	6,280	61	222
Yarrow	65.0	839.2	2,894	103	100
Filter Beds	5.82	—	—	—	—

Total contents . . . 4,105,000,000 gallons.

The positions of the reservoirs and of the principal works connected with them are shown on the Map.

It will be observed that the reservoirs are divided into two groups: the Upper, or Withnell group, consisting of the Upper and Lower Roddlesworth and Rakebrook Reservoirs; and the Lower, or Rivington group, consisting of the Anglezarke and Upper and Lower Rivington Reservoirs. These two groups are connected by a goit or canal 3½ miles long and 21 feet wide.

There are altogether eight reservoirs, and they contain, when full, 4,105,000,000 gallons. Their total surface area at the overflow level is 598 acres, and their total length, measured along the top water lines, is 5½ miles. The total length of the embankments is over 3 miles. The highest embankment is that of the Yarrow (Leicester Vale) Reservoir, which is 103 feet above the bottom of the valley.

The deepest puddle trench is also at the Yarrow Reservoir (Turner's bank). Here the trench had to be carried down to a depth of 167 feet below the natural surface before a solid foundation could be obtained; the total height from the bottom of the foundation to the top of the dam being 257 feet.

Method of Construction

A description of the method of construction adopted at the Yarrow reservoir will apply, practically, to all the Rivington Reservoirs.

A suitable site for the embankment having been selected, a trench was excavated on the centre line of the intended work and carried down to the solid rock right across the valley. This was filled with clay deposited in layers of 9 inches, and carefully puddled so as to produce a homogenous watertight material. This clay wall, having reached the natural surface of the ground, was continued through the embankment, which was also built in thin layers thoroughly rammed and consolidated on both sides of the clay centre.

Before commencing the erection of the embankment all peat and unsound material were stripped from the site.

The inner or water slopes of the embankment have been built to an angle of 3 to 1, and the outer slopes to an angle of 2 to 1.

The impermeability of the dam depends upon the wall of puddled clay in the heart of the dam tied into the solid rock at the bottom and sides of the valley.

The clay wall has been carried up to a batter on each side of 1 inch to every foot vertical, the thickness at the top being 6 feet. The inner slopes of the banks are protected by 15 inch pitching, consisting of the millstone grit of the

Anglezarke and Rivington Reservoirs, as seen from the West Side of Anglezarke.

Rivington Reservoirs: from East Side of Anglezarke. (Yarrow Reservoir on the Left.)

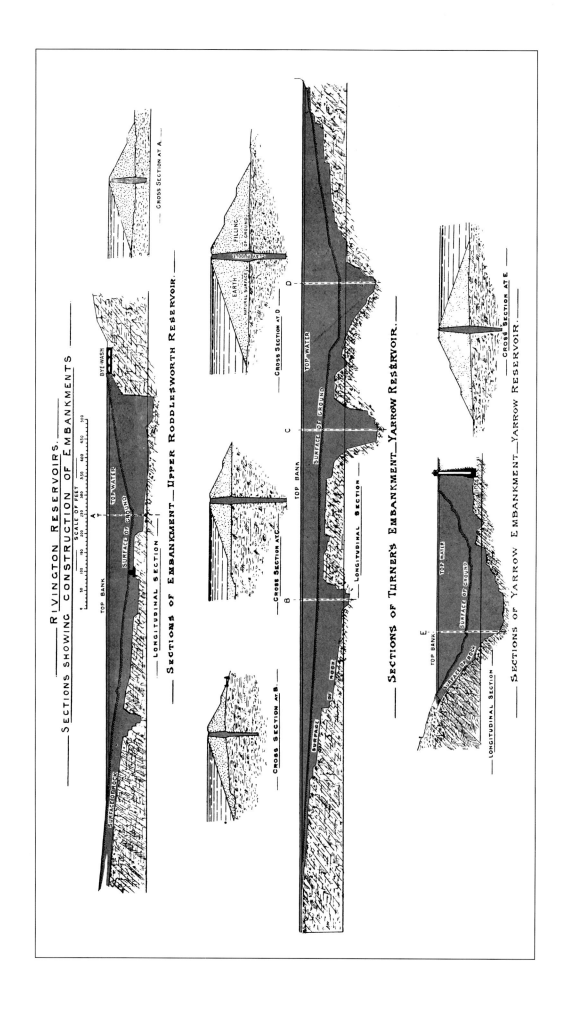

RIVINGTON RESERVOIRS.

— SECTIONS SHOWING CONSTRUCTION OF EMBANKMENTS —

— LONGITUDINAL SECTION —

— SECTIONS OF EMBANKMENT.— UPPER RODDLESWORTH RESERVOIR. —

— CROSS SECTION AT A. —

— CROSS SECTION AT C. —

— CROSS SECTION AT D. —

— CROSS SECTION AT B. —

— LONGITUDINAL SECTION —

— SECTIONS OF TURNER'S EMBANKMENT.—YARROW RESERVOIR. —

— CROSS SECTION AT E. —

— LONGITUDINAL SECTION —

— SECTIONS OF YARROW EMBANKMENT.—YARROW RESERVOIR. —

neighbourhood, laid on a bed of broken stone. The outer slopes have been soiled and grassed over. The outlet from the Yarrow Reservoir is by a tunnel driven through the rock at the side of the valley, and not through the embankment itself as in the earlier reservoirs. The tunnel and valve shaft are both lined with blue bricks.

The bye-wash or overflow is 100 feet wide. The weir and apron and steps are formed of heavy ashlar closely jointed. The pitching forming the bye-wash is of millstone grit, neatly dressed and soundly laid on asphalte concrete. The wing walls are of squared rubble, neatly and closely laid.

Workmanship

All the reservoir embankments and tunnel outlets at Rivington are sound and watertight, and their excellent condition today is evidence of the skill and care exerted in their construction. The water weirs or bye-washes have proved to be of ample capacity for dealing with the largest floods that have been experienced.

Roddlesworth Reservoir

The contents of the Lower Roddlesworth and Rakebrook Reservoirs can only be drawn off by gravitation to the goit, the bottom of which is 10 feet below the top water line of the reservoirs, thus leaving seventy million gallons of water stored which can only be made available for Liverpool by pumping.

When these reservoirs were constructed the whole of their contents were required, and could be utilised by gravitation for compensation purposes, but when the Roddlesworth compensation water was acquired in the year 1867 the reservoirs were not longer used for compensation supplies. On two occasions it has been found necessary, owing to scarcity of water, to pump from below the gravitation level of these reservoirs, once during the drought of 18885 and during another period of dry weather in 1888.

Compensation to the Streams

Compensation water, as provided for by the Liverpool Water Act of 1847, is delivered to the rivers and works affected at the following points:–

>To the Brinscall Mill Print Works, from the goit in Brinscall Village.
>To the Black Brook and White Coppice Mill, from the goit in White Coppice.
>To the Fill Brook from the goit at a point about 14 chains above the inlet to the
>   Anglezarke Reservoir.
>To the River Yarrow, from the foot of the bye-wash, Upper Rivington Reservoir.
>To the River Douglas, from Lower Rivington Reservoir.

Filter Beds

All the water for the supply of Liverpool has to pass into and through the Lower Rivington Reservoir.

From this reservoir the water is drawn off for filtration through sand filters. The original filtration works consisted of six beds, having a total area at the surface of the sand of 182,982 square feet, and two open filtered water tanks, capable of holding 8,384,000 gallons.

In 1870-5 two additional filter beds were constructed. The area of these two beds is 71,302 square feet, making the total filtering area of the eight beds 254,284 square feet. The filtering material consists of 2 feet 6 inches of sand laid on the top of layers of gravel, varying in size from 4 inches diameter to 1/8 inch diameter.

The average rate of filtration during the year 1899 was 2,243,538 gallons per day per acre of sand surface, or 8 1/4 cubic feet per square foot per day.

Purity of Watershed

The Sanitary condition of the watershed and the measures adopted to protect the purity of the supply were very fully described in a report to the Water Committee, dated the 15th November, 1898, which was printed by their instructions.

VIEWS AROUND RIVINGTON EARLY THIS CENTURY

Rivington Pike from George's Lane.

View across Lever Park

Anderton Hall

Ward Hill, Rivington

Red Cot, Rivington

The Street, Rivington

159

The tombs of Lord & Lady Lever at Port Sunlight.

Inside rear cover:
Plan showing proposed alterations to the Bungalow grounds with handwritten instructions from Lord Leverhulme.

Rear cover:
Photographs of the Bungalow grounds, 1998.

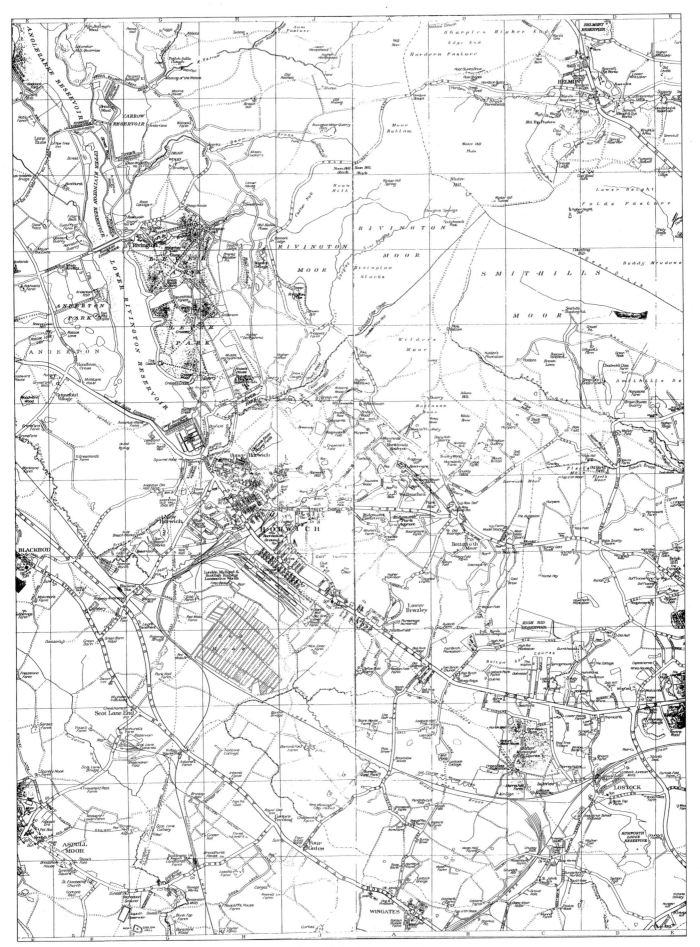

Map of the Rivington area. c.1930

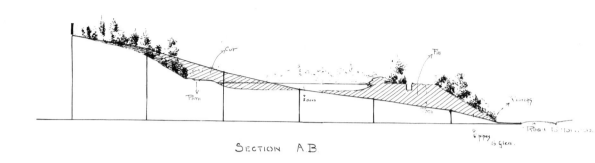

Section A B

Section C. D.

PROPOSED WATER GARDEN
at RIVINGTON BUNGALOW
The Rt Hon Viscount Leverhulme.

Scale of   50 40 30 20 10 0   100   200   feet.